Presents

Shakespeare's Hilarious Tragedies

A play in 4 Acts
Creatively modified by
Brendan P. Kelso

Ensemble cast size:
Minimum of 14 actors, up to 72!

Table Of Contents

Copyright 3

Director's Notes 4

Setting the Stage 5

Prop List 6

Cast of Characters 7

Prologue 11

Julius Caesar 12

Macbeth 34

Romeo & Juliet 60

Hamlet 88

About the Author 117

This play is dedicated to Keagan
who is ALWAYS inspiring me to be creative and silly.

Special thanks to Amy De Friese for inspiring
this play to exist and
Ann Johnson for providing such beautiful artwork

Playing with Plays™ – Shakespeare's Hilarious Tragedies

Copyright © 2004-2024 by Brendan P. Kelso. All rights reserved. Used with permission by
Playing with Plays LLC

No part of this book may be reproduced in any form or by any electronic or mechanical means, including photocopying, recording, information storage or retrieval systems now known or to be invented, without permission in writing from the publisher, except by a reviewer, who may quote brief passages in a review, written for inclusion within a periodical. Any members of education institutions wishing to photocopy part or all of the work for classroom use, or publishers who would like to obtain permission to include the work in an anthology, should send their inquiries to the publisher. We monitor the internet for cases of piracy and copyright infringement/violations. We will pursue all cases within the full extent of the law.

CAUTION: Professionals and amateurs are hereby warned that all plays published by Playing With Plays may be produced only pursuant to a signed written license and are subject to payment of a royalty. The plays are fully protected under the copyright laws of the United States, Canada, the United Kingdom, and all other countries of the Berne Union,. All rights, including dramatic (both amateur and professional), motion picture, radio, television, recitation, public reading, internet, and any method of photographic reproduction are strictly reserved.

Whenever a Playing With Plays play is performed, the following must be included on all programs, printing and advertising for the play: © 2004-2024 by Brendan P. Kelso. All rights reserved. Performed under license from, Playing with Plays LLC, www.PlayingWithPlays.com.

For performance rights please contact:

contact@PlayingWithPlays.com

Cover and poster artwork by
Ann Johnson

Please note, for special circumstances, we do waive copyright and performance fees.
Rules subject to change

www.PlayingWithPlays.com

Printed in the United States of America

ISBN: 9781672837088

Director's Note

Congratulations! You have been given a rare gift of infusing the love of Shakespeare into the minds and hearts of your actors and audience.

I originally wrote Shakespeare for Kids books to open the door for kids to love Shakespeare and his storylines. Over time, and reaching over 100,000 kids, I became aware that not just kids were doing my plays, but teenagers and adults alike. So, the play you read today was born.

If we can make the world of Shakespeare fun, and give a basic understanding of the storyline and characters, then we have done our jobs. His stories, words, and language have weaved themselves into our everyday lives, whether we realize it or not.

The entire point of this play is to inspire the love of Shakespeare into the actors and audience. It is your responsibility, as the director, to make sure you create an environment for this to occur. Creativity is key to melodrama. By creating an open, energetic, and engaging environment, two things happen:

1) The artists care more about the end product and making the show memorable and
2) a performance that the audience will never forget!

This being said, if any actor has a creative interpretation they want to try to help tell the story, then let them try it! That's the beauty of rehearsals, it allows us to continue to try new ideas until something sticks and makes us all laugh.

Lastly, any lines you see highlighted in grey throughout the play are ACTUAL Shakespeare text. So, please don't be TOO creative with these lines! Everything else is fair game!

With these notes, I bid you adieu, break a leg, and most importantly, be creative and have fun!

-Brendan P. Kelso

Setting the Stage

You are doing four 1-act plays in one show, set in four different countries and four different time periods. Knowing that, a common set has to be generic enough to work for all. I have always been a minimalist when it comes to sets, as I like the focus to be on the actors. I use black boxes and minimal props for all my shows. I will occasionally do a backdrop if the actors want it. But, this is entirely up to the director and actors on how elaborate and creative they want to be!

Prop List

Below is a very basic list of props you will need for this performance. It is in no way definitive, as you may be as creative or minimalistic as you like.

BODY COUNTER. This can be any type of counting device you envision: sports score counter with flip numbers, digital score counter (vision a basketball scoreboard maybe?), white board, chalkboard, easel with flip paper, etc. Be creative.

Optional basic prop list for each play:

ALL PLAYS: Swords!

JULIUS CAESAR: Julius Caesar sign, crystal ball, poet's note, "CAESAR IS BAD" letter, "BOO" card, "APPLAUSE" card, money.

MACBETH: Macbeth sign, witch's cauldron, King crown, a message that says, "You Da Man!", Lady Macbeth letter, various creepy ingredients for witch's brew, 2 daggers-not bloody, 2 bloody daggers.

R&J: Napkin and some type of food for narrator after intermission, Romeo & Juliet sign, masquerade masks, thorned flower (Friar), herbal cocktail for Juliet, burger & fries packaging, vial for Romeo (poison).

HAMLET: Hamlet sign, dollar or two, "HAMLET IS RETURNING" letter, skull (we can never forget Yorick!), goblet for poisoned wine, poisoned sword.

CAST of CHARACTERS
JULIUS CAESAR
11 - 17 Actors

Approx Run Time: 20 minutes

¹JULIUS CAESAR: the tyrant dude
²CALPURNIA: Caesar's Wife
MARK ANTONY: ruler after Caesar
⁵OCTAVIUS: ruler after Caesar
BRUTUS: Caesar's ex-friend
CASSIUS: another ex-friend
CINNA: another ex-friend
³DECIUS: another ex-friend
⁵CASCA: another ex-friend
²PORTIA: Brutus' wife
⁴PINDARUS: Cassius' slave
⁴LUCIUS: Brutus' slave
³POMPEY: the first loser to Caesar
⁴SOOTHSAYER: a fortune-teller
³CINNA THE POET: a poet
¹CAESAR'S GHOST: he's a dead Caesar
TOWNSFOLK: townsfolk
HENCHMEN: Pompey's henchmen - they die
NARRATOR: our host - who also plays: Banquo, Tybalt, and Polonius in the other plays

The same actors can play the following parts:
¹CAESAR and GHOST
²CALPURNIA and PORTIA
³POMPEY, CINNA the POET, and DECIUS
⁴SOOTHSAYER, PINDARUS, and LUCIUS
⁵Casca and Octavius can be played by the same actor
Townsfolk can be as many extras as needed or left out

MACBETH
12 - 17 Actors

Run Time: 22 minutes

MACBETH: Thane of Glamis – the good guy, then the bad guy

LADY MACBETH: really evil wife of Macbeth

BANQUO: Macbeth's friend, then ex-friend

[1]WITCHES (#1, 2, & 3): The Weird Sisters with cool lines

ROSS: Thane of Ross

[2]DUNCAN: King of Scotland

MALCOLM: son of King Duncan

DONALBAIN: the other son of King Duncan

MACDUFF: Thane of Fife

[3]LADY MACDUFF: Macduff's wife

[4]SON OF MACDUFF: son of Macduff

[4]CAPTAIN: a captain

MURDERER: a murderer and a really bad guy

[2]SOLDIER: a soldier

[3]SIWARD: an Earl

The same actors can play the following parts:
[1]1-3 witches can be played by 1-3 actors
[2]DUNCAN and SODIER
[3]LADY MACDUFF and SIWARD
[4]CAPTAIN and SON of MACDUFF

ROMEO & JULIET
14 - 18 Actors

Run Time: 21 minutes

THE CAPULETS
LORD CAPULET: Dad Capulet
LADY CAPULET: Mom Capulet
JULIET: the Babe (but a Capulet)
NURSE: Juliet's life-long Nurse
[4]TYBALT: Juliet's cousin
[3]SAMPSON: servant to Capulet
[1]GREGORY: servant to Capulet

THE MONTAGUES
LORD MONTAGUE: Dad Montague
LADY MONTAGUE: Mom Montague
ROMEO: the Dude (but a Montague)
BENVOLIO: Romeo's friend
[2]ABRAM: Montague's servant
[4]BALTHASAR: Romeo's servant

THE COURT
PRINCE ESCALES: the local Prince
[3]MERCUTIO: Romeo's friend
[1]PARIS: wants to marry Juliet

THE CHURCH
FRIAR LAWRENCE: a friar that helps
[2]FRIAR JOHN: a friar that doesn't help

The same actors can play the following parts:
[1]PARIS can also play GREGORY
[2]FRIAR JOHN can also play ABRAM
[3]MERCUTIO can also play SAMPSON
[4]TYBALT can also play BALTHASAR

HAMLET
11 - 20 Actors

Run Time: 25 minutes

HAMLET: son to the dead King Hamlet, nephew to Claudius, the thinker, or "over" thinker (he's complicated)

CLAUDIUS: the big, bad new King of Denmark.

GERTRUDE: Queen, Hamlet's mom, married to his dad & then to his uncle (it's complicated)

[2]POLONIUS: a lord (bad guy too!)

OPHELIA: Polonius' daughter, thinks Hamlet is cute!

LAERTES: Polonius' son and sword-fighter, thinks Hamlet is rotten!

[3]ROSENCRANTZ: crazy guy #1

[3]GUILDENSTERN: crazy guy #2

HORATIO: Hamlet's closest friend

[3]MARCELLUS: Hamlet's friend

[3]BARNARDO: Hamlet's friend

[4]GHOST: a ghost, duh

[4]OSRIC: a young dude

[1]PLAYER 1: an actor

[1]PLAYER 2: another actor

[1]GRAVEDIGGER 1: a person who digs graves

[1]GRAVEDIGGER 2: see above

[2]FORTINBRAS: Prince of Norway

[2]SAILOR: a sailor

ON-LOOKERS: (extras, as many as needed)

The same actors can play the following parts:
[1]PLAYERS and both GRAVEDIGGERS
[2]POLONIUS, SAILOR, and FORTINBRAS
[3]MARCELLUS & BARNARDO can play R & G
[4]GHOST and OSRIC

PROLOGUE

NARRATOR: *(slowly enters and addresses audience)*

All the world's a stage,

And all the men and women merely players:

They have their exits and their entrances;

And each actor today plays many parts.

Welcome to our fun-filled night of Shakespeare tragedies! Yep, you heard me: FUN. TRAGEDIES. Julius Caesar, Macbeth, Romeo & Juliet, and Hamlet. If you haven't figured it out yet, there might be a couple deaths tonight… 33 to be exact, and possibly one or two audience members. We're not sure on that number yet… but, hey… you… *(to an audience member)* yes you! If you use that phone again, we'll know who will be first! Are we clear? Good. Now, enough about us… on with the show!

JULIUS CAESAR
ACT 1 SCENE 1

(Someone walks across stage holding a large sign that says, "JULIUS CAESAR"; to the side, or somewhere visible is a board that says, "BODY COUNT: 0")

NARRATOR: Once upon a time in ancient Rome there was a great battle. *(CAESAR, POMPEY, and 2 HENCHMEN enter fighting)* In this corner, Caesar, and in this corner, Pompey.

POMPEY: Attack!

(NARRATOR does play by play of fight; HENCHMEN attack first and are killed; then POMPEY attacks and is killed; body count is updated)

NARRATOR: And Caesar wins! *(CAESAR exits triumphantly)*

NARRATOR: People are dancing in the streets over Caesar's win.

(TOWNSFOLK cross stage dancing and hollering, saying great things about Caesar; CAESAR, CALPURNIA, BRUTUS, CASCA, CASSIUS, and ANTONY enter)

CASCA: *(to audience)* Peace, ho! Caesar speaks.

CAESAR: Ahh, what a great day Antony, I am now the ruler of Rome!

ANTONY: Yes, Caesar, you are the man. When Caesar says 'do this,' it is perform'd.

CALPURNIA: Caesar, dear, now don't let this go to your head, okay.

CAESAR: Yes, dear. *(enter SOOTHSAYER)*

SOOTHSAYER: *(in a really spooky, creepy voice)* Caesar!

CAESAR: What? Who said my name?

SOOTHSAYER: Beware the Ides of March!

BRUTUS: It is a soothsayer. And I think he is telling you to beware the Ides of March.

CAESAR: What the heck is the Ides of March?

CALPURNIA: It's March 15th, dear.

CAESAR: Whatever.

SOOTHSAYER: *(to the point)* Listen, it means watch your back, or you might find a knife in it!

CAESAR: Huh, that's nice.

SOOTHSAYER: *(in a spooky, creepy voice again)* Beware the Ides of March!

CAESAR: He is a dreamer, let us leave him. *(ALL exit but BRUTUS and CASSIUS)*

CASSIUS: Brutus, I know Caesar is your friend, but this man is now become a god.

(offstage, cries of 'hip-hip-hooray' for Caesar)

CASSIUS: I fear the future of Rome with Caesar in charge.

BRUTUS: Listen, Cassius, Caesar is my friend. What are you worried about?

CASSIUS: You are of the same rank as Caesar, why should that name be sounded more than yours?

BRUTUS: *(confused)* Huh? I've never thought about that!

(CAESAR and ANTONY enter and are downstage away from BRUTUS and CASSIUS)

ANTONY: Caesar, Cassius was acting rather strange earlier.

CAESAR: Yeah, he thinks too much, such men are dangerous and he creeps me out. I don't trust him.

ANTONY: Fear him not, Caesar, he's not dangerous. *(CASSIUS yells and waves his sword around wildly)* Let's get out of here! *(CAESAR and ANTONY exit; CASCA enters)*

BRUTUS: Casca, my friend, what is all the cheering about?

CASCA: Well, Brutus, there was a crown offered to Caesar. They shouted thrice!

CASSIUS: Huh?

CASCA: *(slower to CASSIUS)* THREE TIMES. Antony offered it three times today, but he refused.

CASSIUS: I am telling you, he is trouble!

CASCA: No, the people of Rome like Caesar more because he will not take the crown!

CASSIUS: Yeah, well I still think he is trouble.

BRUTUS: Why don't you come over later and we will talk about it. *(BRUTUS exits)*

CASSIUS: *(to audience)* Well, Brutus, thou art noble. Hmmm, I must think of an evil plan to deceive Brutus and turn him against Caesar. *(looks at CASCA)* Hey, Casca, we need to take down Caesar!

CASCA: *(shrugs shoulders)* Okay. It's greek to me why you want to do this, but okey-dokey!

(ALL exit laughing evilly)

ACT 1 SCENE 2

NARRATOR: *(referencing Casca and Cassius)* They don't seem very nice. The word on the streets is that Cassius has recruited other people to conspire against Caesar. Cassius is working with Cinna, another conspirator, on his plot to turn Brutus against Caesar. *(enter CASSIUS and CINNA)*

CASSIUS: Cinna, listen, my friend; Let's win the noble Brutus to our party. Take this paper to Brutus. Once he reads this cleverly crafted evil letter, he will join us!

CINNA: Okay, boss.

(ALL exit)

ACT 2 SCENE 1

NARRATOR: *(enter BRUTUS)* Brutus is hanging out in his orchard. It is three in the morning. Three in the morning? Why are you not asleep, better yet, why am I not asleep? Anyway, he hasn't slept since Caesar got back in town.

BRUTUS: What, Lucius ho!

(enter LUCIUS)

LUCIUS: Yes, sir!

BRUTUS: Lucius, my servant, I am afraid Caesar might use his new-found power in a bad way. If he does, that would be a terrible thing!

LUCIUS: That would be bad, very bad. *(enter CINNA)*

CINNA: *(hands letter to BRUTUS)* Hey, Brutus, here is a letter from Cassius.

BRUTUS: *(reads letter)* "Caesar is bad." That's it!

It must be by his death. Speak, strike, redress!

Shall Rome stand under one man's awe? What, Rome?

O Rome, I make thee promise, I will resolve to kill Caesar to save Rome from what he might do.

LUCIUS: Hey, just a reminder, tomorrow is March 15th.

BRUTUS: Well wouldn't you know it, the Ides of March! Now I am going to do a very bad thing, I must

Hide it in smiles and affability:

I must think him as a serpent's egg.

Which, hatched, would as his kind grow mischievous,

And kill him in the shell.

LUCIUS: *(looking at the words on the letter)* Wow, that was a really persuasive letter.

(enter CASSIUS, CASCA, and DECIUS)

CASCA: So?

BRUTUS: I'm in! *(they high-five each other and cheer 'conspirators!')*

NARRATOR: *(to audience)* What you see before you is the group of conspirators against Caesar.

LUCIUS: *(to audience)* Not me! I'm outta here!

(LUCIUS exits)

CASSIUS: Great. This is Decius. He is a conspirator against Caesar as well.

BRUTUS: He is welcome too.

DECIUS: Hello.

CASCA: This, Casca; and this, Cinna.

BRUTUS: They are all welcome.

DECIUS: Shall no man else be touched but only Caesar?

CASCA: Hey, I think we need to kill Antony too.

BRUTUS: Antony? Nah, he's a wimp.

ANTONY: *(offstage)* Hey!

BRUTUS: *(to ANTONY)* Mind your own business! Don't you have an Egyptian queen to woo or something? *(to CASSIUS)* Don't worry about him.

CASSIUS: I am worried whether Caesar will come forth today or no, for he is superstitious grown of late.

DECIUS: Never fear that. If he be so resolved, I can o'ersway him. I will go over to Caesar's house and bring him to the capitol tomorrow morning. I will deceive him.

CASSIUS: Great! We'll leave you, Brutus. Let's laugh evilly as we exit! *(ALL exit, laughing evilly, except BRUTUS; PORTIA and LUCIUS enter)*

NARRATOR: The wife!

PORTIA: Brutus my lord. You have been a real pain since yesterday. What's up?

BRUTUS: Portia! What mean you? Wherefore rise you now? Ahhh…I'm not feeling good? *(LUCIUS shaking head behind BRUTUS)*

PORTIA: Nice try. Now tell me why you are up this late. You suddenly arose and walked about.

BRUTUS: Indigestion? I'm not well in health, and that is all. *(LUCIUS shaking head behind BRUTUS)*

PORTIA: You used that one last night. Why won't you tell me the truth? Who were those visitors that were just here?

BRUTUS: Trick or Treaters? *(LUCIUS tries again, but BRUTUS quickly looks back)*

PORTIA: It's March. Look, I love you, but you are buggin' me. Now go to bed!

BRUTUS: *(to audience)* O ye gods! Render me worthy of this noble wife! *(to PORTIA)* Yes, dear. *(BRUTUS exits)*

PORTIA: Lucius, I want you to follow Brutus tomorrow and tell me what he is up to. Bring me word, boy, if thy lord look well.

LUCIUS: Okay. *(PORTIA and LUCIUS exit)*

ACT 2 SCENE 2

NARRATOR: The next morning, at Caesar's house. *(CAESAR enters)*

CAESAR: My wife is freaking me out. Last night thrice hath Calpurnia screamed in her sleep, 'Help ho, they murder Caesar!' *(CALPURNIA enters)*

CALPURNIA: Caesar, I have a bad feeling about today.

CAESAR: Yeah, I know, you woke me up. Okay, see ya!

CALPURNIA: You shall not stir out of your house today.

CAESAR: Cowards die many times before their deaths, The valiant never taste of death but once.

CALPURNIA: *(demanding)* You will stay here as I say!

NARRATOR: The wife has an iron fist!

CAESAR: I am not afraid of death. *(to audience)* Now, my wife, that's something else. Okay, I'll stay. *(enter DECIUS)*

DECIUS: Caesar, all hail! Good morrow, worthy Caesar.

CAESAR: Hello, Decius.

DECIUS: I come to fetch you to the Senate House.

CAESAR: Ohh, um…I'm not going today.

DECIUS: What? But everybody is waiting for you.

CAESAR: Yeah, well, my wife had this bad dream and kept saying, 'Help ho, they murder Caesar' and it really gave me the creeps, and that soothsayer yesterday, too.

DECIUS: Is that what your wife said? No, no, no. This dream is all amiss interpreted. It was a vision fair and fortunate. It means if you DON'T come and help, they will murder you. You have to come. The Senate is going to crown you today.

CAESAR: Crown? Did you say, "crown"?

DECIUS: Yeah, crown to mighty Caesar. A nice shiny crown.

CAESAR: Well, why didn't you say so? Let's go! *(DECIUS and CAESAR exit)*

CALPURNIA: You should listen to me! Bye, dear! *(CALPURNIA exits)*

NARRATOR: She tried to warn you!

ACT 3 SCENE 1

NARRATOR: Later that day. The capitol.

(CAESAR, BRUTUS, LUCIUS, CASSIUS, DECIUS, CINNA, CASCA, and SOOTHSAYER enter)

CAESAR: *(to Soothsayer)* The Ides of March are come. *(mocking Soothsayer and dancing around)* And look at me, I'm still here! Neener, neener, neener!!!

SOOTHSAYER: Ay, Caesar, but not gone. In other words, continue watching your back, buddy!

CAESAR: Whatever, I will be crowned today!

SOOTHSAYER: You should listen to my warning.

(CONSPIRATORS are slowly circling Caesar)

NARRATOR: *(to Caesar)* Would you listen to the soothsayer?

CAESAR: Be quiet, narrator. You are not even part of the story. *(to audience, proudly)* I am constant as the northern star.

NARRATOR: Sorry.

CAESAR: *(suddenly noticing everyone around him)* Why are you guys all around me with those funny looks on your faces? And all of those sharp swords pointed at…….me.

SOOTHSAYER: I'm outta here! Tried to warn you!

(SOOTHSAYER exits; ALL start stabbing CAESAR)

CAESAR: *(to audience after some stabbing)* This really hurts. *(to BRUTUS)* Et tu, Brute! *(ALL stop)*

BRUTUS: Huh? What does that mean?

CAESAR: It's Latin for 'You too Brutus?' Sheesh!

BRUTUS: Oh…..yeah. *(BRUTUS delivers final blow)*

NARRATOR: *(to Caesar)* I told you to listen to the Soothsayer! *(CAESAR flashes sword at NARRATOR as he finally dies; TOWNSFOLK run across stage screaming in pandemonium)* There is pandemonium on the streets!

CASSIUS: Well we did it. We have freed Rome!

CINNA: Liberty! Freedom! Tyranny is dead!

BRUTUS: Let's all cry, 'Peace, freedom, and liberty!' Here comes Antony.

Welcome, Mark Antony!

(ANTONY enters, updates body count board, and kneels next to Caesar; LUCIUS exits)

ANTONY: O mighty Caesar! Dost thou lie so low? What did you guys do here? What a mess!

BRUTUS: Caesar was my friend, but I did this for Rome!

NARRATOR: Nice friend.

(BRUTUS glares and shows sword at narrator who quickly hides behind podium)

ANTONY: You do realize that you just started a civil war?

CASCA: Hmmm. *(asking CASSIUS)* Did we think about that?

(CASSIUS shakes head 'no'; ALL exit, CAESAR left on stage)

ACT 3 SCENE 2

NARRATOR: *(to audience)* Later that day, Caesar's funeral, and you are all Romans at the funeral. This is where we have interactive theater, so please join along to make it more fun!

(ANTONY, BRUTUS, CASSIUS, CINNA, and DECIUS enter; TOWNSFOLK enter audience area)

CASSIUS: Brutus, a word with you. I don't trust letting Antony speak at Caesar's funeral.

BRUTUS: Don't worry, I have it under control.

CASSIUS: You know not what you do.

BRUTUS: I will myself into the pulpit first,

And show the reason of our Caesar's death.

(addresses audience) Dear Romans, I know it looks bad that we murdered Caesar, but it is not that I loved Caesar less, but that I loved Rome more. Had you rather Caesar were living, and die all slaves, than that Caesar were dead, to live all free men? That is why he needed to kick the bucket.

(NARRATOR shows 'boo' card to audience)

BRUTUS: Now please, listen to your new leader, Antony.

ANTONY: *(addresses audience)*

Friends, Romans, countrymen, lend me your ears;

I come to bury Caesar, not to praise him.

The noble Brutus hath told you Caesar was ambitious and an honourable man. But truth be told, Brutus is wrong! Caesar wasn't a bad guy.

(TOWNSFOLK say things like, "O noble Caesar", "O woeful day", "O most bloody site", "we will be revenged")

TOWNSFOLK: The will, the will, we will hear Caesar's will!

ANTONY: You will compel me then to read the will? If you have tears, prepare to shed them now. Listen, this is how good Caesar was: in his will, he left all of you money! YOU get Caesar's money and YOU get Caesar's money. EVERYONE gets Caesar's money!

(ANTONY throws money into the audience; NARRATOR shows 'applause' card to audience)

ANTONY: So, I think revenge is in order!

TOWNSFOLK: Most noble Caesar, we'll revenge his death!

(NARRATOR starts the 'revenge' chant, BRUTUS and CASSIUS flash swords at NARRATOR, but after seeing the hostile audience, BRUTUS and CASSIUS flee the scene; TOWNSFOLK say things like, "we will burn the house of BRUTUS", "Away then, come, seek the conspirators" TOWNSFOLK exit)

BRUTUS: I am leaving Rome!

CASSIUS, DECIUS, CINNA: Me too!

(BRUTUS, CINNA, DECIUS, and CASSIUS exit)

ACT 3 SCENE 3

NARRATOR: This is where trouble starts to happen. Enter the innocent bystander.

(enter TOWNSFOLK and CINNA THE POET who is reading a poem on a sheet of paper)

TOWNSFOLK: Hey, what is your name? Aren't you Cinna the conspirator against Caesar?

CINNA THE POET: Nope, I am Cinna the Poet.

NARRATOR: He happens to have the same name as one of the conspirators, poor chap.

TOWNSFOLK: We think you are one of the conspirators against Caesar. Tear him to pieces!!! *(they kill CINNA THE POET)*

CINNA THE POET: NOOOOOOOOOOOOOOO! Don't you know it, I am Cinna the poet! *(dying in extreme agony)*

(NARRATOR gets body offstage; updates body count)

ACT 3 SCENE 4

(LUCIUS and PORTIA enter)

PORTIA: Did you follow Brutus?

LUCIUS: Yep

PORTIA: So?

LUCIUS: Well, Brutus killed Caesar and then skipped town when the townsfolk started getting mad and saying something like: "We will burn the house of Brutus."

PORTIA: Hey, that's this house. Wait, do you smell smoke?

LUCIUS: Yeah, I'm outta here! *(LUCIUS exits)*

PORTIA: This is bad, very bad, not good.

(PORTIA exits)

ACT 4 SCENE 1

NARRATOR: Well it is really getting tense on the streets now. People are screaming for justice to what the conspirators did to Caesar. Meanwhile, Antony meets with Octavius, another new ruler of Rome, and they are preparing for war against Brutus and Cassius. Speaking of Brutally Brutus and Careless Cassius, they are currently at their wits' end in Brutus' tent.

(enter BRUTUS and CASSIUS, very mad at each other; LUCIUS follows)

CASSIUS: Brutus, most noble brother, you have done me wrong and that makes me very mad at you.

BRUTUS: What did I do? How should I wrong a brother? You were the one who tricked me into killing Caesar with that letter! You are very greedy and corrupt, the same reason we killed Caesar! The name of Cassius honours this corruption.

CASSIUS: *(very mad)* Don't talk to me that way. It hurts my feelings.

BRUTUS: You have a very bad temper… and bad breath.

NARRATOR: Hello. *(getting their attention)* Hi, yes, I have a friend that is a shrink. Maybe he can help. His phone number is…… *(starts talking until he sees CASSIUS and BRUTUS glaring and pointing swords at him)*

CASSIUS: What is it with this guy?

BRUTUS: I don't know. Maybe we should kill him? *(they hold swords at throat of NARRATOR)*

NARRATOR: Whoa…..Hey, listen, I know where I am not wanted. Let me just go back to storytelling. Right over there. *(NARRATOR quickly makes his way back to the podium)*

CASSIUS: Now, where were we? Oh yes, you're right, I do have a bad temper. I feel bad about it. Would you kill me? *(tries to hand his sword to BRUTUS)*

BRUTUS: No, now we have work to do. *(PORTIA screams offstage)*

CASSIUS: What was that?

BRUTUS: I think that was my wife's scream.

(PORTIA runs on stage and dies)

BRUTUS: Huh, that was my wife and she just killed herself from guilt and stress. Portia is dead.

CASSIUS: Bummer. Sorry, good buddy.

BRUTUS: That's okay. Hey, Narrator, make yourself useful and clean this up.

NARRATOR: My job is to tell stories and that's it! *(CASSIUS and BRUTUS quickly point swords and glare at him)* Okay, okay. *(gets body offstage; updates body count)* I didn't sign up for this! Now that they are buddy-buddy, they start plotting how to take on Octavius and Antony. Cassius leaves Brutus to go to sleep.

CASSIUS: Good night, my lord.

BRUTUS: Good night, good brother. *(CASSIUS exits)* Hey, Lucius, play me some music.

LUCIUS: Nah, I'm tired. *(goes to sleep)*

BRUTUS: Lazy slave.

(CAESAR'S GHOST enters)

BRUTUS: Ha! who comes here? Aghhhhh! Speak to me, who are you?

CAESAR'S GHOST: Thy evil spirit, Brutus. I am the ghost of Caesar. You are a very bad man.

BRUTUS: Go away.

CAESAR'S GHOST: Okay.

(ALL exit)

ACT 5 SCENE 1

(BRUTUS and CASSIUS enter from one side of the stage and OCTAVIUS and ANTONY from the other side)

NARRATOR: The battlefield. Octavius and Antony happen to run into Brutus and Cassius in the immense combat zone.

ANTONY: *(shoves aside NARRATOR)* Make forth, the generals would have some words.

BRUTUS: Words before blows; is it so, countrymen? Very wisely threat before you sting.

ANTONY: Don't 'countrymen' me, you villains! *(shoves BRUTUS)*

OCTAVIUS: Enough! I draw a sword against conspirators. Which one of you killed Caesar?

(BRUTUS and CASSIUS point at each other)

ANTONY: They both did.

OCTAVIUS: I am here to avenge Caesar's death, if you dare fight today. I will fight till Caesar's three and thirty wounds be well avenged. So which one of you wants to die first?

(BRUTUS and CASSIUS point at each other)

CASSIUS: You know, this is my birthday, so you should kill him first.

BRUTUS: Man, you are ruthless.

CASSIUS: Hey, every man for himself. *(CASSIUS and BRUTUS run offstage for their lives)*

ANTONY: Don't you hate chickens?

(ALL exit chasing)

ACT 5 SCENE 2

NARRATOR: Well, this is just getting ugly. Let's see, according to our man on the field, there are some battles taking place just outside of Rome. It looks as if Octavius' army is getting weak, but we just got confirmation that Cassius' soldiers have fled the scene in the middle of the battle.

(enter CASSIUS and PINDARUS)

CASSIUS: Pindarus, my slave, this just doesn't look good.

PINDARUS: Nope, really doesn't. You need to Fly further off, my lord, fly further off!

Mark Antony is in your tents, my lord

Fly, therefore, noble Cassius, fly far off.

CASSIUS: This hill is far enough. Are those my tents on fire?

PINDARUS: Yep, they are, my lord.

CASSIUS: Well, this stinks. My life is run his compass.

PINDARUS: What?

CASSIUS: I need to die.

PINDARUS: Oh.

CASSIUS: O, coward that I am, would you kill me?

PINDARUS: Sure, but do I get to go free after you're gone?

CASSIUS: Yes! Now be a free man. *(hands sword to Pindarus)*

PINDARUS: Great! So I am free! *(takes sword and stabs him; Then runs offstage not sure of what he just did, but stops to update body count)*

CASSIUS: Caesar, thou art revenged, even with the sword that killed thee. *(CASSIUS dies)*

NARRATOR: Ouch, that looks like it hurt. *(BRUTUS enters)*

BRUTUS: Ahhhh man. He is slain. O Julius Caesar, thou art mighty yet. *(to audience)* A moment of silence, please. *(no time passes)* Okay, now back to the battle. *(BRUTUS exits)*

ACT 5 SCENE 3

NARRATOR: Okay, well I just got word that Brutus' army is getting knocked around pretty bad by Antony's army. So bad that Brutus' wants to take his own life but can't find anyone to do it. *(enter BRUTUS)*

BRUTUS: *(to narrator)* Hey, do you mind killing me?

NARRATOR: No, I am the narrator; I am not part of the story.

BRUTUS: Yeah, you sure didn't act like it during the play.

NARRATOR: Don't start getting brave with me.

BRUTUS: You know, I have nothing to lose, and you are buggin' me. *(kills NARRATOR and then holds up 'applause' sign to audience; updates body count)*

BRUTUS: Now, where was I? Oh yes, *(stabs himself)* farewell. Caesar, now be still; I killed not thee with half so good of will. *(BRUTUS updates body count, then dies)*

(enter OCTAVIUS and ANTONY)

OCTAVIUS: Well, looks as if our work is done here. I feel bad for Brutus.

ANTONY: Yeah, Brutus was the noblest Roman of them all. He was the only man who was doing what he thought was best for Rome. All the conspirators, save only he, did what they did in envy of great Caesar.

OCTAVIUS: Ok, enough about Caesar and Rome. Hey, I know. Let's go to Scotland. My cousin, Macbeth, lives there!

ANTONY: Sweet! Maybe we can get these togas in plaid…

(ALL exit)

MACBETH

(Someone walks across stage holding a large sign that says, "MACBETH" with an "X" through MACBETH, and below scribbled in, "The Scottish Play")

ACT 1 SCENE 1

(WITCHES enter to thunder and lightning)

WITCHES: Fair is foul, and foul is fair; Hover through the fog and filthy air.

WITCH #1: When shall we three meet again? In thunder, lightning, or in rain?

WITCH #2: When the hurlyburly's done, When the battle's lost and won.

WITCH #3: Wow, talk about confusion. What did we just say?

WITCH #2: I dunno.

WITCH #1: Let's meet again after the war to talk with Macbeth.

WITCHES #3 & #2: Oh…Okay.

(WITCHES exit)

ACT 1 SCENE 2

(DUNCAN, MALCOLM, and DONALBAIN enter)

DUNCAN: Malcolm, my son, I wonder what is going on with the war?

MALCOLM: I don't know, your highness, but look, here comes a random wounded young captain. Maybe he knows?

(CAPTAIN enters)

CAPTAIN: *(bloody and delirious, kneels)* King of Scotland. There was lots of blood and bodies. The Thane of Cawdor is a traitor. But we were saved for brave Macbeth, well he deserves that name, killed them all and chased the Norwegians out of Scotland! ALL HAIL MACBETH! *(as he falls on his face and dies a miserable death; body count updated)*

DONALBAIN: Awesome. *(DONALBAIN steps over body to talk to DUNCAN)* Hey Dad, here comes the worthy Thane of Ross.

(ROSS enters, steps over body)

DUNCAN: Great. Ross, go tell Macbeth that he is now the Thane of Cawdor.

ROSS: I'll see it done.

DUNCAN: What he hath lost, noble Macbeth has won. And get rid of this body!

ROSS: Yes, sir! *(ALL exit, ROSS gets CAPTAIN'S body offstage)*

ACT 1 SCENE 3

(WITCHES enter and gather around the cauldron; WITCHES do various creepy and gross things)

WITCHES: The weird sisters, hand in hand,

Posters of the sea and land,

Thus do go, about, about,

Thrice to thine, and thrice to mine,

And thrice again, to make up nine.

WITCH #1: Wow, we really are weird chicks.

WITCH #2: Yeah, and filled with itchy ticks.

WITCH #3: Shhh!!! You two lunatics!

A drum, a drum; Macbeth doth come.

(enter MACBETH AND BANQUO)

BANQUO: You're my good buddy, Macbeth.

MACBETH: Mine too, Banquo.

BANQUO: Friends forever!

MACBETH: Yeah! *(they high-five or do some other special handshake; MACBETH starts looking around)* So foul and fair a day I have not seen.

BANQUO: Look at these crazy looking old hags. What are these, so withered and so wild in their attire?

MACBETH: Yeah, they're pretty creepy *(sniffs one)* and smelly too! Speak if you can: what are you?

WITCHES: Hey, Macbeth!

MACBETH: Yeah?

WITCH #1: All hail Macbeth, hail to thee, Thane of Glamis!

WITCH #2: All hail Macbeth, hail to thee, Thane of Cawdor!

WITCH #3: All hail Macbeth, that shalt be king hereafter! Of Scotland that is!

BANQUO: That was cool! Speak then to me, I want you to tell me my future, too!

WITCH #1: Lesser than Macbeth, and greater.

WITCH #2: Not so happy, yet much happier.

WITCH #3: All your sons will be kings, though thou be none.

BANQUO: Well, that makes no sense. Wait, yes it does?

MACBETH: Dude! Your children shall be kings!

BANQUO: You shall be king.

MACBETH: Right!? And the Thane of Cawdor too! But, I am only the Thane of Glamis, and if chance will have me king, why, chance may crown me.

WITCHES: Bye-Bye! *(WITCHES vanish)*

BANQUO: Whoa! Where did they go? Whither are they vanished? *(looking around)* Look, here comes the worthy Thane of Ross.

(ROSS enters)

MACBETH: Hey, Ross.

ROSS: Hello. The king hath happily received, Macbeth, the news of thy success. He wants me to give you this message…. *(reads from a very long sheet)* "You da man." *(shows sheet to audience)* Seriously, it says "YOU DA MAN."

MACBETH: You da man? What does that mean?

ROSS: It means, since you saved our country, the king bade me call thee Thane of Cawdor and you get all of his goods.

BANQUO: Say what? Can the devil speak true? Are you serious?

ROSS: Yep!

MACBETH: *(aside to audience)* Really....hmmm, those old ladies were right, two truths are told, Glamis, and Thane of Cawdor. I wonder what it would be like to be King. I wonder what I would have to do to be King.... oh this could be fun! Come what may.

BANQUO: Mac, what are you thinking over there?

MACBETH: Oh, nothing. *(said with a big fake smile)*

(ALL exit)

ACT 1 SCENE 4

(Enter DUNCAN, MALCOLM, DONALBAIN, MACBETH, and BANQUO)

DUNCAN: Well hello, my NEW Thane of Cawdor.

MACBETH: Hello, King!

DUNCAN: Just want to let you all know, that I am pronouncing my son Malcolm to be the next King when I step down.

MALCOLM: Yes!

MACBETH: *(aside)* No!

DUNCAN: What?

MACBETH: Nothing. Nothing at all…

DONALBAIN: Good job, brother.

MACBETH: *(aside to audience)* The Prince of Cumberland, too? I must o'erleap, for in my way it lies. Now I have to go through the king and his son. Man, this is going to get messy.

BANQUO: Mac, what are you thinking over there?

MACBETH: Oh, nothing, *(said with a big fake smile)* and don't think I'm thinking anything either!

(ALL exit)

ACT 1 SCENE 5

(LADY MACBETH enters)

LADY MACBETH: *(reading letter)* "Dear honey, met some really weird old ladies. They said, "Hail, king that shalt be." Cool, huh? See ya soon, bye." Hmmmmmm....... Macbeth is too full o'th'milk of human kindness to do what needs to be done. *(to audience)* Yep... you all know what needs to be done... don't you? *(thinking to herself evilly as she walks offstage)* Must be mean, must be nasty, cruel, callous, evil, vicious, wicked, malicious.......oh yeah, and did I mention GORGEOUS!

(LADY MACBETH exits)

ACT 1 SCENE 6

(MACBETH enters; LADY MACBETH is center)

MACBETH: Hi, Honey, I'm home! Guess what, King Duncan comes here tonight.

LADY MACBETH: *(to audience)* Sweet, just in time to put my evil master plan to work! *(to MACBETH)* Great Glamis, worthy Cawdor, I have a plan for you to be king! *(as she snickers evilly)*

MACBETH: Okay.

LADY MACBETH: Since the king's coming over for dinner, I will be serving him a large helping of "your goose is cooked," if you know what I mean. *(using air quotes)*

MACBETH: *(confused)* Ahhh. No, I don't know what you mean.

LADY MACBETH: I am going to serve him his "last meal." If you know what I mean.

MACBETH: Right! *(confused)* Wrong, I don't know what you mean.

LADY MACBETH: *(frustrated)* I am going to serve him food and you are going to kill him. Do you NOW know what I mean?

MACBETH: Right!

(LADY MACBETH and MACBETH laugh together evilly and make evil faces towards the audience; there is a loud knocking)

LADY MACBETH: That's the king. Remember, look like the innocent flower, but be the serpent under't. Now, put on a happy face and let's go!

(both exit)

ACT 1 SCENE 7

(MACBETH, LADY MACBETH, DUNCAN, MALCOLM, DONALBAIN, BANQUO are all sitting around eating dinner)

DUNCAN: Great meal, Lady Macbeth. You have to send me that recipe.

BANQUO: That really was a great meal.

DONALBAIN: It sure was!

LADY MACBETH: Well, I am glad you enjoyed it. Oh my, look at the time. *(yells)* Now, everyone, go to sleep! *(LADY MACBETH shoos everyone out of the room)*

ALL: Okay.

ACT 1 SCENE 8

MACBETH: *(to himself alone on stage)* To be or not to be......whoops, wrong play. To kill or not to kill..... there we go....if I kill him lots of people will hate me, BUT, if I kill him I will be King. Vaulting ambition or my conscience... Hmmmm, to kill or not to kill... Oh, we teach bloody instructions, which being taught, could return to plague th'inventor...who happens to be ME! Hmmmm, to kill or not to kill... *(LADY MACBETH enters)*

LADY MACBETH: So, did you do it?

MACBETH: *(taking a stand)* I have decided that I am not going to do it. We will proceed no further in this business. He has honoured me of late, and I have bought golden opinions from all sorts of people!

LADY MACBETH: WHAT!? I see you now to look so green and pale. Yet earlier, you were my brave husband who was going to be the King of Scotland! Are you a man? Get on with it!

MACBETH: I dare do all that may become a man; who dares do more is none.

LADY MACBETH: Fine! Have a great life with these "golden opinions" from all sorts of people. And live a coward in thine own mind! Ya wimp!

MACBETH: *(whining)* But, what if we should fail?

LADY MACBETH: We fail? Screw your courage to the sticking-place, and we'll not fail! When Duncan is asleep, I'll get his guards drunk, and we can blame them! Now, pull yourself together and go do the deed.

MACBETH: Yes, dear. *(as LADY MACBETH puts the daggers in his hands and shoves him offstage)*

ACT 2 SCENE 1

(DUNCAN runs onstage and dies with a dagger stuck in him, MACBETH gets his body offstage and then returns with the bloody daggers and updates the body count; LADY MACBETH enters)

LADY MACBETH: Did you do it?

MACBETH: *(clueless)* Do what?

LADY MACBETH: KILL HIM!

MACBETH: Oh yeah, all done. I have done the deed. Did thou not hear a noise?

LADY MACBETH: No, just an owl scream. Go get some water and wash this filthy witness from your hand. *(pointing at the daggers)* What are those?

MACBETH: What?

LADY MACBETH: Why did you bring these daggers from the place?

MACBETH: Ummmmm, I don't know.

LADY MACBETH: Well go put them back!

MACBETH: NO! I'll go no more! I'm scared of the dark, and there is a dead body in there. I am afraid to think what I have done.

LADY MACBETH: Man you are a wimp. Give me the daggers… *(as she's exiting)* Why do I have to do everything myself?! *(LADY MACBETH takes the daggers, exits, and returns)*

LADY MACBETH: All done.

(there is a loud knock at the door)

LADY MACBETH: It's 2 am! This really is not a good time for more visitors. *(goes to the door)* Who is it? *(opens door)*

MACDUFF: It is Macduff. I am here to see the king. Is thy master stirring? He did command me to call timely on him.

MACBETH: He is sleeping in there.

(MACDUFF exits while MACBETH and LADY MACBETH look at each other)

MACDUFF: *(offstage scream)* AGHHHHHHHHHH!!! *(MACDUFF enters)* O horror, horror, horror. He's dead, he's dead!!!

MACBETH: Who?

MACDUFF: Who do you think? Most sacrilegious murder! Murder and treason! Banquo and Donalbain! Malcolm, awake!

BANQUO: *(BANQUO, MALCOLM, and DONALBAIN enter)* What happened? Can't someone get a good night sleep around here?

MACDUFF: O Banquo, Banquo, our royal master's murdered.

MALCOLM & DONALBAIN: Aghhhhhhh!!!!!!!!

DONALBAIN: We must be next.

MALCOLM: Let's get out of here. I'll to England.

DONALBAIN: To Ireland, I. There's daggers in men's smiles. I'm scared!

(MALCOLM and DONALBAIN exit)

MACDUFF: Well, since there is no one left to be King, why don't you do it Mac?

LADY MACBETH & MACBETH: Okay. *(LADY MACBETH, MACBETH and MACDUFF exit)*

BANQUO: *(to audience)*

Thou hast it now, King, Cawdor, Glamis, all,

As the weird women promised, and I fear,

Thou play'dst most foully for't. *(MACBETH returns)*

MACBETH: Bank, what are you thinking over there?

BANQUO: Oh, nothing. *(said with a big fake smile)* Gotta go! See ya! *(BANQUO exits)*

MACBETH: I don't trust Banquo, he knows too much. *(towards offstage)* Hey, Murderer!

MURDERER: *(MURDERER enters)* Yes, sir?

MACBETH: Banquo. *(makes slash across throat sign)*

MURDERER: Gotcha. *(MURDERER exits)*

MACBETH:

It is concluded. Banquo, thy soul's flight,

If it find heaven, must find it out to-night.

(MACBETH exits laughing evilly)

ACT 3 SCENE 1

(BANQUO is standing on stage tying his shoe or something like that; MURDERER enters)

MURDERER: Hey, you Banquo?

BANQUO: Yeah, who are you?

MURDERER: Murderer.

BANQUO: Uh oh. *(BANQUO is stabbed)* O, treachery!

(BANQUO dies; MURDERER updates body count while laughing evilly)

ACT 3 SCENE 2

(MACBETH, LADY MACBETH, and BANQUO'S GHOST enter; BANQUO'S GHOST sits among the audience)

MACBETH: Sweet remembrancer! What are you doing here?

LADY MACBETH: I am your wife. I live here.

MACBETH: No! Him!!! *(accusing audience)* Which of you have done this?

LADY MACBETH: What, my good lord?

MACBETH: Do you not see Banquo's ghost right there!

LADY MACBETH: Yeah, ok…. *(addressing audience)* Sit, worthy friends. His fit is momentary; upon a thought, he will again be well. *(slaps MACBETH)* Hey, pull it together! *(BANQUO'S GHOST slowly exits)*

MACBETH: Honey, I am really going wacky over all of this killing, greed, and guilt. What am I supposed to do?

LADY MACBETH: Oh my gosh, have we not already gone over this! Are you a man?

MACBETH: Right. What's done is done, there is no turning back now, and I will kill anyone that comes in my way! I will tomorrow go and see those crazy witches! More shall they speak!

(MACBETH and LADY MACBETH exit)

ACT 4 SCENE 1

(WITCHES enter with Cauldron)

WITCH #1: Round about the cauldron go;
In the poisoned entrails throw.

WITCHES: Double, Double toil and trouble,
Fire burn, and cauldron bubble.

WITCH #1: Eye of newt, and toe of frog,
Wool of bat, and tongue of dog.

WITCH #2: Scale of dragon, tooth of wolf,
Witches' mummy, maw and gulf.

WITCH #3: Adder's fork, and blind-worm's sting,
Lizard's leg, and howlet's wing.

WITCHES: Double, Double toil and trouble,
Fire burn, and cauldron bubble.

WITCH #3: By the pricking of my thumbs,
Something wicked this way comes.

(enter MACBETH)

MACBETH: How now, you secret, black, and midnight hags! *(WITCHES glare at MACBETH)* Ahhh, I mean lovely, beautiful, and so very thoughtful sisters! Tell me what I need to know!

WITCH #1: Speak.

WITCH #2: Demand.

WITCH #3: We'll answer.

WITCH #2: Say, if thou'dst rather hear it from our mouths, or from our masters'?

MACBETH: Quit talking in riddles, you weird sisters! Just tell me!

WITCH #1: Macbeth, Macbeth, Macbeth, beware Macduff.

WITCH #2: None of woman born shall harm Macbeth.

WITCH #3: Macbeth shall never die until the Great Birnam Wood comes to High Dunsinane Hill.

MACBETH: So let me get this straight: a forest that is miles away from a hill has to actually move together, nobody born by a woman can harm me, and I only have to beware of Macduff?

WITCHES: Yep. That's what we said. Don't you listen?

(WITCHES exit)

MACBETH: *(to himself)* Cool. First I have to kill Macduff and his family! Man, this show is just getting bloody.

(MACBETH exits)

ACT 4 SCENE 2

(Enter ROSS, LADY MACDUFF, and SON OF MACDUFF)

LADY MACDUFF: Ross, what had my husband done, to make him fly the land? His flight was madness. I'm really a bit angry with him because he left us behind like this.

ROSS: Lady Macduff, I just want you to know that your husband, Macduff, has headed to England to try and save Scotland. He is noble, wise, judicious, and best knows.

SON OF MACDUFF: Mom, I thought you said dad was a traitor and left us?

LADY MACDUFF: I guess I was wrong!

ROSS: Oh, by the way, danger does approach you nearly. You should leave soon, and I mean VERY soon. Bye! *(ROSS exits)*

LADY MACDUFF: Why should I fly? I have done no harm. Don't worry. We will leave soon.

(enter MURDERER)

MURDERER: Hello.

LADY MACDUFF: What are these faces? Who are you?

MURDERER: Murderer.

SON and LADY MACDUFF: Uh oh. *(LADY MACDUFF and SON run offstage in opposite directions; MURDERER chases LADY MACDUFF; a loud scream is heard; LADY MACDUFF stumbles on stage and dies; SON enters from opposite side and dies; MURDERER updates body count laughing evilly)*

(ROSS enters; MURDERER glares at ROSS while exiting)

ROSS: Ouch, that looked like it hurt. I tried to warn you. I think I will go tell Macduff about this. Boy, is he going to be bummed.

(ROSS exits, getting LADY MACDUFF and SON offstage)

ACT 4 SCENE 3

(Enter MACDUFF and MALCOLM)

MACDUFF: Malcolm, we need to have you come back to Scotland so you can be king. I am not treacherous.

MALCOLM: Yeah, but Macbeth is bloody, luxurious, avaricious, false, deceitful, sudden, malicious, smacking of every sin that has a name! Oh, he makes my blood boil!!! On top of all that, I hear he is being a bully and a tyrant.

MACDUFF: Let it out buddy, let it out… But, guess what? I got the King of England to let me borrow his army so we can go over and kick Macbeth's butt.

MALCOLM: Great! Let's do this!

(enter ROSS)

MALCOLM: Hello, Ross.

MACDUFF: Hey, how's my family?

ROSS: Macbeth.

MACDUFF: No!

ROSS: Yes.

MACDUFF: AGGGHHHHHHHHHHHHHH!!!!!!!!!!

(MACDUFF runs of stage screaming and waving his sword)

MALCOLM: Wow, that's a bummer.

ROSS: Yeah.

(ROSS and MALCOLM exit)

ACT 5 SCENE 1

(enter LADY MACBETH sleep-walking)

LADY MACBETH: *(in sleep-walking voice)* Can't wash blood off hands. Out damned spot! Out, I say! Will these hands ne'er be clean? Feel guilty about King Duncan, Banquo, Lady Macduff. Husband going nuts. *(repeats constantly until she exits; as she exits, she says the next line)* To bed, to bed, to bed!

ACT 5 SCENE 2

(enter MACBETH talking to himself)

MACBETH: I have to kill everyone. No one will stop me from being King.

(enter SOLDIER – scared)

SOLDIER: Umm, sir?

MACBETH: What do you want, soldier?

SOLDIER: Well, the weirdest thing has happened. It appears that Birnam Woods is moving closer to our castle here on Dunsinane Hill. Oh yeah, and all of your army guys are scared of you and are deserting their posts.

(A loud scream from LADY MACBETH is heard offstage)

MACBETH: Wherefore was that cry?

SOLDIER: Oh, the queen, my lord, is dead. Lady Macbeth just died. *(LADY MACBETH enters, updates body count, then dies on stage)*

MACBETH: Bummer. *(To himself)*

Out, out, brief candle!

Life's but a walking shadow, a poor player

That struts and frets his hour upon the stage

And then is heard no more.

Eh, she was bugging me anyway.

SOLDIER: Huh?

MACBETH: Guess you can't win them all. Oh, by the way, soldier.

SOLDIER: Yes? *(MACBETH kills soldier)* Ouch! Why did you do that? You're never supposed to kill the messenger!

MACBETH: Oh, sorry about that. Just, didn't like all the news you told me.

SOLDIER: Oh. *(falls over dead; MACBETH updates body count)*

MACBETH: *(to himself)* Well, the witches have been right every time. But I think they are wrong this time. I will die fighting!

(enter Siward)

MACBETH: What do you want, Young Siward?

SIWARD: I want to kill you, Macbeth!

MACBETH: Funny you say that, thou wast born of woman, and I can't be killed by a man born from woman. Any last words?

SIWARD: Two… Uh oh.

(MACBETH kills Siward; updates body count)

MACBETH: This is going to be easy.

(enter MACDUFF)

MACDUFF: Tyrant, show thy face!

MACBETH: Well, well, well.

MACDUFF: That's a deep subject.

MACBETH: I will have you know that I bear a charmed life which must not yield to one of woman born. In other words, I cannot be killed by a man born from woman.

MACDUFF: Really? That's nice.

MACBETH: *(taken aback)* Why do you say that?

MACDUFF: Because, Macduff was from his mother's womb untimely ripped.

MACBETH: What???? Now wait a minute here, you were still technically "born" correct? The witches specifically said, "born."

MACDUFF: Well, yeah...but according to Shakespeare, I was "untimely ripped."

MACBETH: *(complaining)* Wait, what!?!? What does that even mean? Born...ripped...I mean, you exist, right?!

MACDUFF: Witches are tricky, man, what can I say? It was like a riddle. It's not my fault you trusted some smelly old ladies in the middle of the forest with your fate.

MACBETH: Huh?

MACDUFF: What the witches REALLY meant was no man NATURALLY born from a woman. *(pauses)* Stinks to be you.

MACBETH: Oh, NOW I get it... well then, it does stink to be me!

MACDUFF: Great, then yield thee, coward. My voice is in my sword. Any last words?

MACBETH: Mommy?

(MACDUFF kills MACBETH; updates body count)

MACDUFF: Hey, Malcolm!

(MALCOLM, DONALBAIN, and ROSS enter)

DONALBAIN: Got him!

ROSS: *(talking to Malcolm)* Well, you're King now!

MACDUFF: Hail, King of Scotland.

EVERYONE: Hail, King of Scotland.

MALCOLM: Great! Since you were all so brave my thanes and kinsmen, henceforth be earls! *(EVERYONE cheers)* Oh, and I have one more proclamation to say; It's intermission time! And, most dear actors, eat no onions or garlic, for we are to utter sweet breath; and I do not doubt but to hear them say, it is a sweet comedy. No more words: Away! Go, Away! *(addresses audience)* Come, join us, for a great feast in the lobby.

(MALCOLM and DONALBAIN high-five while everyone cheers; ALL exit)

INTERMISSION

(enter NARRATOR eating some type of food with a napkin half-stuck in his collar)

NARRATOR: *(dressed as Tybalt)* Well, wasn't that feast fantastic! The turkey legs were delicious! *(looking at an audience member)* What? You didn't get one? Eh, stinks to be you! Anyway, let's revisit where we are; we've been to Rome and Scotland, and now we are headed back to Italy…Verona to be exact! Did you know that nine of Shakespeare's plays were based in Italy? And, let's see, our body count is currently at…16, and I've died twice myself! I'm getting the feeling they don't like me much around here! But, shhhhh here come the Montagues and Capulets…

(Someone walks across stage holding a large sign that says, "Romeo & Juliet")

ROMEO & JULIET

PROLOGUE

(Montagues enter, face audience, and say, "Montagues"; then Capulets enter and say, "Capulets", then they stand back; they briefly glare, growl, and yell at each other; they form a semi-circle and address audience)

ROMEO: Two households, both alike in dignity,

JULIET: In fair Verona, where we lay our scene,

PARIS: From ancient grudge break to new mutiny,

FRIAR LAWRENCE: Where civil blood makes civil hands unclean.

FRIAR JOHN: From forth the fatal loins of these two foes

PRINCE: A pair of star-cross'd lovers take their life

MERCUTIO: Whose misadventured piteous overthrows

NURSE: Doth with their death bury their parents' strife.

TYBALT: The fearful passage of their death-marked love,

LORD CAPULET: And the continuance of their parents' rage,

LADY CAPULET: Which but their children's end, nought could remove,

LORD MONTAGUE: Is now the two hours', achmmm….20 minutes', traffic of our stage;

LADY MONTAGUE: The which if you with patient ears attend,

PRINCE: What here shall miss, our toil shall strive to mend. *(ALL exit)*

ACT 1 SCENE 1

(enter SAMPSON and GREGORY)

SAMPSON: Hey, Gregory.

GREGORY: What's up, Sampson?

SAMPSON: I really don't like those Montagues. But, you know what I LOVE?

GREGORY: What?

SAMPSON: I love fighting them! *(they break out in fake swordplay)*

GREGORY: Yeah, we are so much better than they are. The quarrel is between our masters, and us their men.

(enter ABRAM, not noticing the other two)

GREGORY: Draw thy tool, here comes one of the house of Montague. Go beat him up.

SAMPSON: Okay. Hey you! Yeah, you ugly….ahhh…I mean Montague.

ABRAM: Capulets! You don't know when to stop, do you? Do you bite your thumb at me, sir?

SAMPSON: I do bite my thumb, sir. Draw, if you be men.

(they are about to fight when BENVOLIO enters)

BENVOLIO: Part, fools! We really shouldn't be fighting. Put up your swords. *(aside)* Not like you know what to do with them anyway.

GREGORY: Oh look, another Montague.

(enter TYBALT)

SAMPSON: Hey Tybalt, the Montagues don't want to fight. They're babies!

TYBALT: What? A Montague? Turn thee, Benvolio, look upon thy death. Let's go!

(they are about to fight)

BENVOLIO: *(drawing his sword)* Guys, we really shouldn't be fighting. I do but keep the peace.

TYBALT: What! Drawn and talk of peace? I hate the word, as I hate hell, all Montagues, and thee. Have at thee coward!

(they fight)

(enter LADY and LORD CAPULET from one side of the stage; enter LADY and LORD MONTAGUE from the other side of the stage)

LORD CAPULET: My sword, I say! Old Montague is come.

LADY CAPULET: Go get them, dear!

LORD MONTAGUE: Thou villain Capulet! Hold me not, let me go.

LADY MONTAGUE: *(to LADY CAPULET)* You want some of me?!

(Lord and Ladies start to fight; PRINCE enters)

PRINCE: Rebellious subjects, enemies to peace. Will they not hear? What ho, you men, you beasts! *(as loud as possible)* STOP!!!!!! *(They all stop and go to their appropriate side)* This is the third time you disturbed the quiet of MY streets, and I am really getting tired of it. If ever you disturb our streets again, your lives shall pay the forfeit of the peace. Clear?

ALL: Clear.

TYBALT: Ahhhh, sorry but it's not clear to me, and probably not clear to them. *(points at audience)* I don't understand.

PRINCE: If you start a fight again, I will kill you – Clear? *(TYBALT nods)* Good, now, on pain of death, all men depart. *(no one leaves)* Go!

(ALL exit except BENVOLIO, LORD, and LADY MONTAGUE)

LADY MONTAGUE: Benvolio, O where is Romeo? Saw you him today?

BENVOLIO: No, Lord and Lady Montague, my friend has been avoiding me.

LORD MONTAGUE: He has been acting rather strange lately. Teenagers!

LADY MONTAGUE: Find out what is wrong with him, OK?

BENVOLIO: Will do. I will know his grievance!

(LORD and LADY MONTAGUE exit; ROMEO enters)

BENVOLIO: Romeo, Romeo! Good morrow, cousin.

ROMEO: Benvolio, there is this really cool girl, Rosaline. I mean, she's cute! Anyway, I like her a lot. But I am out of her favour. What do I do?

BENVOLIO: Don't worry about her. There are other fish in the sea. Examine other beauties.

ROMEO: Other beauties? You might as well teach me how I should forget to think. But hey, I hear she is going to a big party tonight. Should we go?

BENVOLIO: Yes, and I will show you other girls more beautiful than she. Like her! Right there in the audience! *(points at audience member)* And I will make thee think thy swan a crow.

ROMEO: You're on!

(ALL exit)

ACT 1 SCENE 2

(enter LORD CAPULET and PARIS)

PARIS: Lord Capulet, what say you to my suit? I like your daughter, Juliet. Can I marry her?

LORD CAPULET: Paris, buddy, listen. My daughter is only 13, she has not seen the change of fourteen years. She can't even drive yet! Why don't you wait about two more years and then we will talk.

PARIS: Pleeeeeease. Pretty please.

LORD CAPULET: Hmmm. Well, I am having this really cool party tonight. Why don't you come, and if Juliet likes you and says yes, then, why not!

PARIS: Awesome!

(ALL exit)

ACT 1 SCENE 3

(enter LADY CAPULET, NURSE, JULIET)

LADY CAPULET: Nurse, where's my daughter? Call her forth to me.

NURSE: JULIET!

JULIET: How now, who calls?

LADY CAPULET: My daughter, the valiant Paris seeks you for his love and thinks you are really cute.

NURSE: I have been your nurse all your life Juliet, and I believe you should think about this guy.

LADY CAPULET: How stands your disposition to be married? Because he is very good looking. Can you love the gentleman?

JULIET: If I like him, I will think about it.

NURSE: Great! Let's go to the party!

(ALL exit)

ACT 1 SCENE 4

(enter ROMEO, MERCUTIO, BENVOLIO wearing masks)

BENVOLIO: Mercutio, are you sure that by wearing these masks we will be safe at a Capulet party?

MERCUTIO: No problem. They will have no clue.

ROMEO: Well here we are. But I don't see Rosaline.

BENVOLIO: I told you, look at the other girls.

ROMEO: Yeah, yeah. Love is just too rough.

MERCUTIO: You need to laugh my friend. If love be rough with you; be rough with love.

ROMEO: Leave me alone.

(enter LORD and LADY CAPULET, JULIET, TYBALT, NURSE, and other maskers all dancing and having a fun time)

ROMEO: *(seeing Juliet for the first time)*

What lady is that, which doth enrich the hand

Of yonder knight?

MERCUTIO: No clue, man.

ROMEO: *(to himself)*

O she doth teach the torches to burn bright!

TYBALT: *(noticing Romeo)*

This, by his voice, should be a Montague.

'Tis he, that villain Romeo. I must get my rapier.

LORD CAPULET: Tybalt, don't pick a fight, let him alone.

TYBALT: What?! Aghhhh…. I will get him later. *(TYBALT exits)*

ROMEO: *(to Juliet)* Hey, you're cute.

JULIET: So are you.

NURSE: Juliet, your mother wants to talk to you.

(JULIET walks over to talk to LADY CAPULET)

ROMEO: What is her mother?

NURSE: Her mother is the lady of the house, Lady Capulet.

ROMEO: *(very dramatic to audience)* Oh nooooo. My mom is going to be bummed. I just fell in love with a Capulet.

(ALL exit except JULIET and NURSE)

JULIET: Come hither, Nurse. What is yond gentlemen?

NURSE: What?

JULIET: Who was the cute guy?

NURSE: Oh…

His name is Romeo, and a Montague;

The only son of your great enemy.

JULIET: *(very dramatic to audience)* Uh oh, that's trouble. I just fell in love with a Montague, a loathed enemy. Oh well, what's the worse that could happen?

(ALL exit)

ACT 2 SCENE 1

(enter ROMEO and JULIET)

ROMEO: *(seeing JULIET)*

But, soft! What light through yonder window breaks?

It is the east, and Juliet is the sun.

JULIET: Ay me!

ROMEO: *(overwhelmed by her words)*

She speaks!

O speak again, bright angel!

JULIET:

O Romeo, Romeo! Wherefore art thou Romeo?

Deny thy father and refuse thy name;

Or if thou wilt not, be but sworn my love,

And I'll no longer be a Capulet.

What's in a name? That which we call a rose

By any other name would smell as sweet.

ROMEO: *(aside)* She is my sworn enemy, but look at her. WOW, she's cute!

See, how she leans her cheek upon her hand!

O that I were a glove upon that hand,

That I might touch that cheek!

(ROMEO is in a daze)

JULIET: O Romeo, Romeo! Hello! HEY, ROMEO!

ROMEO: Oh yeah, sorry. Just daydreaming over here. Hey, I love you.

JULIET: And I love you.

NURSE: *(offstage)* Juliet!

JULIET: Gotta go! Dear love, adieu!

(JULIET exits)

ROMEO: OH. MY. GOSH! She LOVES me!!!! WOW!!!

(JULIET enters)

JULIET: Hey Romeo, I'm back!

ROMEO: HELL-O again! Oh, I got an idea. Let's get married!

JULIET: Wow, you move fast.

ROMEO: I know what I want!

NURSE: *(offstage)* Madam!

JULIET: Ok, sounds awesome! But, I have to go. My nurse is really feisty. *(melodramatically)* A thousand times good night!

(JULIET exits blowing kisses melodramtically)

ROMEO: *(to audience)* A THOUSAND TIMES! 1…2…3… *(big happy sigh)* Wait a minute. It's night time. Being in night, could all this be but a dream? Must wake self up… *(starts trying to wake himself up; JULIET enters; ROMEO is still facing audience)*

JULIET: Hist, Romeo, hist! I will send my nurse tomorrow to find the time and place of our marriage.

ROMEO: SWEET! Your voice is like softest music to attending ears!

JULIET: Ahh, you're so sweet!

NURSE: *(offstage, really loud and demanding)* JULIET!!!

JULIET: Ok, I really must leave this time.

Good night, Good night! Parting is such

sweet sorrow,

That I shall say good night till it be morrow.

(JULIET exits, humming, "Going to the chapel and we're gonna get married…")

ROMEO: (to audience) Whoa! She is AMAZING, am I right? I need to go talk to Friar Lawrence to figure out this marriage thing.

(ROMEO exits)

ACT 2 SCENE 2

(enter FRIAR LAWRENCE)

FRIAR LAWRENCE: Ah, what a beautiful morning. *(picks up a plant and pricks his finger)* Ouch! Plants, like people, can be both good and evil.

(enter ROMEO)

FRIAR LAWRENCE: Romeo, what brings you here today?

ROMEO: I have a small request, and it's just slightly complicated. *(pauses)* I want to get married to Juliet.

FRIAR LAWRENCE: *(outraged)* The Capulet!

ROMEO: Yeah. My heart's dear love is set on hers, so hers is set on mine.

FRIAR LAWRENCE: *(still outraged)* Holy Saint Francis, are you crazy!

ROMEO: But I am in love.

FRIAR LAWRENCE: *(very calm)* Well, okay. This might turn your households and end the feud between the Montagues and the Capulets.

ROMEO: Awesome!

(ALL exit)

ACT 2 SCENE 3

(enter MERCUTIO and BENVOLIO)

MERCUTIO: Benvolio, where the dev'l should this Romeo be?

BENVOLIO: *(joking)* Hey, Mercutio, he's probably still in love with Rosaline. Here comes Romeo.

(ROMEO enters)

ROMEO: Hey guys!

MERCUTIO: *(teasing Romeo)* Still in love with Rosaline?

ROMEO: Well now that you mention it …

(enter NURSE)

NURSE: So what's the plan?

MERCUTIO: *(very sarcastic)* Hey Romeo, now SHE'S better than Rosaline.

NURSE: *(to Romeo)* What saucy merchant was this, that was so full of himself?

ROMEO: Ignore him, he's just a gentleman that LOVES to hear himself talk. Tell Juliet we will get married this afternoon at Friar Lawrence's.

NURSE: Okay.

(ALL exit)

ACT 2 SCENE 4

(enter FRIAR LAWRENCE, ROMEO, JULIET)

JULIET: My Nurse told me to meet you here to be married.

FRIAR LAWRENCE: Are you ready?

ROMEO: Ready.

JULIET: Ready.

FRIAR LAWRENCE: Okay, all done. You're married. You can now kiss the bride.

ROMEO: Sweet! *(goes in for the kiss; JULIET stops him)*

JULIET: Wait! My family is right there.

ROMEO: Oh.

FRIAR LAWRENCE: Okay, fine. You can hug, then.

(ROMEO and JULIET look at each other and decide to hug instead)

FRIAR LAWRENCE: *(to audience)* They just got married! Let's hear it for them! *(FRIAR gets audience to clap)* Maybe this IS a Shakespeare comedy after all!

JULIET: *(as they are exiting)* Shhh! We can kiss backstage!

FRIAR LAWRENCE: Teenagers!

(ALL exit)

ACT 3 SCENE 1

(enter BENVOLIO and MERCUTIO; enter TYBALT from opposite side)

TYBALT: *(angry)* Where's Romeo?

MERCUTIO: You want some of me?

TYBALT: No, I want Romeo.

(enter ROMEO)

ROMEO: My good friends.

TYBALT: Bring it on, Romeo. Thou art a villain.

ROMEO: I will not fight you.

MERCUTIO: *(wanting to fight)* Come on, Romeo.

ROMEO: No, I have my reasons.

BENVOLIO: We should listen to Romeo.

MERCUTIO: Fine, I'll fight him.

TYBALT: Bring it on!

(MERCUTIO and TYBALT fight)

ROMEO: NO!

(TYBALT stabs MERCUTIO)

ROMEO: Good Mercutio!

MERCUTIO: A plague o' both your houses. I am sped.

(MERCUTIO dies)

ROMEO: Nooooooooooo, Mercutio! Aghhh….Tybalt, I'm really upset. I mean really, REALLY upset. *(pulling his sword out)*

BENVOLIO: Whoa, Romeo. Do you see that guy? *(pointing at dead MERCUTIO)* Do you want to be like him?

TYBALT: Oh yeah he does!

ROMEO: What?!

(ROMEO and TYBALT fight, TYBALT is killed)

BENVOLIO: Romeo, away, be gone!

(ROMEO exits; enter PRINCE, LORD and LADY CAPULET and MONTAGUE)

PRINCE: What in the world happened here? Why are there dead bodies on the ground all over MY streets? Who began this bloody fray? Huh?

BENVOLIO: Well, Tybalt, here slain, killed Mercutio, *(BENVOLIO updates body count)* and then Romeo's hand did slay Tybalt. *(updates body count again)*

PRINCE: And for that offence, immediately we do exile him hence. Romeo is banished from Verona. And clean up this mess!

(ALL exit; BENVOLIO gets bodies offstage)

ACT 3 SCENE 2

(enter ROMEO and FRIAR LAWRENCE)

ROMEO: Friar, I did a bad thing.

FRIAR LAWRENCE: Yeah, I heard. Not too good of you. Nice job turning this comedy back into a tragedy. Oh, and the prince says you are to be banished from Verona.

ROMEO: Nooooooooooooo! Be merciful, say 'death'. Do not say 'banishment'! I will never be able to see my Juliet again! Heaven is here, where Juliet lives.

(ROMEO falls on the ground crying, very melodramatic; NURSE enters)

NURSE: O holy Friar, where's my lady's lord? Where's Romeo?

(FRIAR points to the ground)

NURSE: Oh, yeah, pretty obvious and a bit pathetic. Hey, lover boy. Juliet is pretty bummed. She weeps and weeps.

ROMEO: Noooooooooooo!

(ROMEO tries to stab himself, failing miserably; NURSE takes sword away)

FRIAR LAWRENCE: Why don't you go see Juliet, and then leave town.

ROMEO: *(excited)* Great idea!

(ALL exit)

ACT 4 SCENE 1

(enter ROMEO and JULIET)

JULIET: Oh Romeo! Wilt thou be gone?

ROMEO: Oh Juliet! It is almost morning, and I must leave.

JULIET: Do you have to?

ROMEO: I must be gone and live, or stay and die. And I really prefer the going and living thing.

(NURSE enters)

NURSE: Whoa, you're still here? You better leave soon, and when I say "soon" I mean NOW! *(NURSE shoves out ROMEO)*

(ROMEO exits and LADY and LORD CAPULET enter)

LADY CAPULET: Oh, by the way, Juliet, your dad says you have to marry Paris.

JULIET: I don't want to.

LORD CAPULET: WHAT!? You green-sickness carrion, you disobedient wretch! You will do what I say!

JULIET: FINE!

LORD CAPULET: GOOD! *(to audience)* That was easy!

(ALL exit but JULIET)

JULIET: I need to talk with Friar Lawrence, to know his remedy.

(enter FRIAR LAWRENCE)

FRIAR LAWRENCE: You called?

JULIET: Wow, that was fast. I want to stay with Romeo. What can I do?

FRIAR LAWRENCE: No problem. Take thou this vial. The roses in thy lips and cheeks shall fade. You will look like you are dead. When they take you to the morgue, your Romeo will be there waiting. Then you will awake as from a pleasant sleep.

JULIET: Give me, give me!

FRIAR LAWRENCE: Just hold on a second. *(calling offstage)* Friar John!

(FRIAR JOHN enters)

FRIAR JOHN: Yes.

FRIAR LAWRENCE: I need you to send a message to Romeo.

FRIAR JOHN: Okay.

(FRIAR JOHN exits)

FRIAR LAWRENCE: *(calling offstage)* FRIAR JOHN!

(FRIAR JOHN enters)

FRIAR JOHN: Yes?

FRIAR LAWRENCE: You don't know what the message is.

FRIAR JOHN: Oh. Well, what is it?

FRIAR LAWRENCE: Tell Romeo to meet Juliet at the tomb tomorrow evening.

FRIAR JOHN: Okay.

(FRIAR JOHN exits)

FRIAR LAWRENCE: Go home, be merry, drink up, and good luck!

(FRIAR LAWRENCE gives vial to JULIET then exits)

JULIET: Farewell, dear father. To drink, or not to drink, that is the question. Romeo, Romeo, Romeo! Here's drink, I drink to thee.

(JULIET drinks potion; to audience) Tasty! *(Passes out; NURSE enters)*

NURSE: Rise and shine, my dear mistress, what mistress! Juliet! I must needs wake you. Lady, lady, lady! Wake up!!! JULIET! NOOOOOOO. Alas, alas! Help, help! My lady's dead!

(LADY and LORD CAPULET, FRIAR LAWRENCE, and PARIS enter)

ALL: Aghhhhh....

LORD CAPULET: My daughter!

FRIAR LAWRENCE: *(to himself)* Wow, that was quick.

LORD CAPULET: What?

FRIAR LAWRENCE: *(badly faking a cough)* I said, I feel sick. Now we need to take her to the tomb.

(They pick up JULIET, and carry her offstage; ALL exit)

ACT 5 SCENE 1

(enter ROMEO and BALTHASAR)

ROMEO: *(very happy)* How now, Balthasar, my servant, the day is beautiful! How are you today?

BALTHASAR: *(hesitating)* Well...

ROMEO: I'm glad you're feeling well!

BALTHASAR: Hmmm...I'm feeling, okay.

ROMEO: Only okay, but the day is beautiful! Enough about you. Do you have any news from Verona, how doth my Juliet? For nothing can be ill, if she be well!

BALTHASAR: Yeah, about that. I have bad news. Really bad news.

ROMEO: Really, no good news?

BALTHASAR: Nope.

ROMEO: Not even just a little.

BALTHASAR: Nope, nada, and no.

ROMEO: What's the bad news?

BALTHASAR: Juliet is dead.

ROMEO: NOOOOOOO......I am going to get some poison and kill myself tonight in her tomb. Juliet, I will lie with thee tonight.

(ALL exit)

ACT 5 SCENE 2

(enter FRIAR JOHN and FRIAR LAWRENCE)

FRIAR LAWRENCE: Hello, Friar John. Welcome from Mantua. Were you able to deliver the letter? What says Romeo?

FRIAR JOHN: Well, I tried, but it just didn't happen, so I got a burger and fries instead. Want one?

FRIAR LAWRENCE: What! That's not good. Unhappy fortune! Poor Juliet, closed in a dead man's tomb. I have to go save them!

(ALL exit)

ACT 5 SCENE 3

(JULIET is lying dead on the ground; enter ROMEO)

ROMEO: I will open her tomb and kill myself next to my dear love Juliet!

(enter PARIS)

PARIS: My dear Romeo Montague, what are you doing here, disturbing a Capulet? I am putting you under arrest! I do apprehend thee.

ROMEO: This is a bad time, Paris. Tempt not a desperate man. Fly hence and leave me.

PARIS: I do defy thy conjuration, and apprehend thee for a felon here.

ROMEO: *(confused)* What?! Will thou provoke me? Then have at thee, boy!

(they fight; ROMEO kills PARIS)

PARIS: O, I am slain! Open the tomb, lay me with Juliet. *(PARIS dies melodramatically)*

ROMEO: *(to PARIS' dead body)* Yeah, that's not going to happen. *(to Juliet)* O Juliet, how I love you so. Here's to my love! *(Drinks poison)* Hmmmm, tastes like soda. *(or drink of choice)* Thy drugs are quick. Thus with a kiss I die. *(ROMEO dies)*

(enter FRIAR LAWRENCE)

FRIAR LAWRENCE: *(to audience)* Oh shoot, I am too late. The lady stirs.

(JULIET awakes)

JULIET:

O comfortable Friar, where is my lord?

Where is my Romeo?

FRIAR LAWRENCE: Yeah, about that, well there was a slight problem with the plan. *(points at ground)*

JULIET: NOOOOOOOOOO!

FRIAR LAWRENCE: I hear people coming. Let's go! I'll put you in a sisterhood of holy nuns, you'll be totally safe! Come go, good Juliet, I dare no longer stay.

(FRIAR LAWRENCE updates body count then exits)

JULIET:

What's here?

Poison I see hath been his timeless end.

Bummer, he left none for me, no friendly drop.

(noises outside) Then I'll be brief. O happy dagger…

(ROMEO hands dagger to JULIET)

JULIET: Thank you.

O happy dagger!

This is thy sheath; there rust, and let me die.

(JULIET dies and falls on ROMEO)

(enter PRINCE, LORD CAPULET, LORD MONTAGUE, and FRIAR LAWRENCE)

PRINCE: What misadventure is so early up? Why are there MORE dead bodies on MY streets?!

LORD CAPULET: My daughter is dead.

LORD MONTAGUE: My son, too.

PRINCE: I will investigate and find out what happened here!

FRIAR LAWRENCE: I think I might know.

PRINCE: Then say at once what thou dost know in this. Tell us or die!

FRIAR LAWRENCE: Whoa! Okay, okay….. I will be brief. You see she liked him, he liked her, they got married.

LORD CAPULET and LORD MONTAGUE: WHAT!!!

FRIAR LAWRENCE: Anyway, they got married, Juliet faked dying; Romeo didn't know, that was the one thing that went wrong, and killed himself over her loss; she found out and killed herself over her loss of him. And now we stand here over the dead bodies.

PRINCE: *(to the LORDS)* Capulet, Montague? See what a scourge is laid upon your hate. Look what your quarreling has accomplished. Your two children are dead.

LORD CAPULET: Wow, I was wrong to act this way the entire time.

LORD MONTAGUE: Me too. Let's be friends!

(they hug)

(enter CLAUDIUS who starts a slow clap and updates body count)

CLAUDIUS: *(to audience)* Ok, this is getting way too sappy for me. Gross. *(to the LORDS)* Hey guys, yeah you, why don't you follow me to Denmark, where I can show you how to be a great dictator... ahhh, I mean ruler!

PRINCE: Excuse me, Claudius, but you're in Hamlet, not in Romeo & Juliet. Do you mind?

CLAUDIUS: Yeah, I know, but, do you see that audience member yawning? This is starting to get BOOOORRRRING!!!

PRINCE: Well, that may be, but my streets are finally peaceful! For never was a story of more woe, than this of Juliet and her Romeo.

CLAUDIUS: Oh blah, blah, prose, prose... Fine, I'm outta here! *(to audience)* Time to overthrow a kingdom and get my evil on!

(ALL exit; Someone walks across stage holding a large sign that says, "OMELETTE" with an "X" through OMELETTE, and below scribbled in, "HAMLET")

Notes

HAMLET

ACT 1 SCENE 1

(enter BARNARDO, HORATIO, and MARCELLUS)

MARCELLUS: Guys! Guess what? I have seen a ghost twice before!

HORATIO: No you haven't, have you?

BARNARDO: Yep! It's true. I have seen him too!

HORATIO: You guys are just pulling my leg!

(enter GHOST sneaks up behind HORATIO)

GHOST: Boo!

(HORATIO screaming frantically; meanwhile, MARCELLUS and BARNADO are laughing)

MARCELLUS: Is it not like the King?

BARNARDO: Yes, it looks like Hamlet's dad, just a touch more… oh, I don't know…. pale?

HORATIO: Ohhhh, that ghost is NOT a good thing. It's scary! Smells bad, too. Bad things will happen! I mean, listen to his voice, it's creepy. *(GHOST makes creepy noises)*

BARNARDO: So what should we do?

HORATIO: We must tell Hamlet! He'll know what to do!

MARCELLUS and BARNARDO: Good idea!

(ALL exit)

ACT 1 SCENE 2

(enter CLAUDIUS and GERTRUDE)

CLAUDIUS: *(to the audience)* I love being the ruler! *(HAMLET enters)* Hey, Hamlet, my new son, why are you looking so down in the dumps?

HAMLET: *(to audience while pointing at Claudius)* A little more than kin, and less than kind. *(to Claudius)* Oh, I'm just bummed that my dad died and my mom married my uncle the very next day…ohh, excuse me…I mean YOU!

GERTRUDE: Dear, stop being such a drag. All that lives must die. You know… the circle of life, or haven't you heard?

HAMLET: Whatever, Mom.

That it should come to this!

He is my father's brother, but no more like my father

Than I to Hercules!

I'm going to see my friends.

(GERTRUDE, CLAUDIUS exit; HORATIO, MARCELLUS, and BARNARDO enter)

HORATIO: Hamlet, I saw your dad last night as a ghost!

HAMLET: No way!

BARNARDO and MARCELLUS: Way!

HAMLET: I thought I saw him in a dream the other night, in my mind's eye. I'll stop by tonight and check it out!

(ALL exit)

ACT 1 SCENE 3

(LAERTES, OPHELIA, and POLONIUS enter)

LAERTES: Ophelia, sis, please stop hanging out with Hamlet. That prince is a bit crazy.

OPHELIA: But I love him!

LAERTES: Whoa, remember, this is a tragedy, not a fairy tale. Most people die in tragedies, especially people who love the main character. Did you not watch the previous plays? Macbeth, Caesar, Romeo and Juliet… where are they now? Dead I tell you!

POLONIUS: Laertes, aren't you supposed to be going back to France?

LAERTES: Oh yeah! See ya, Dad! *(LAERTES exits)*

POLONIUS: *(to LAERTES as he leaves)* Hey! Neither a borrower nor a lender be!

LAERTES: What?

POLONIUS: Just giving you some advice about money! But remember this above all: to thine own self be true!

LAERTES: *(a bit confused)* Oh. Okay. Later!

POLONIUS: *(to OPHELIA)* Your brother is right. Hamlet is crazy.

OPHELIA: But, I so totally like him!

POLONIUS: I forbid you to see him!

OPHELIA: I shall obey, Dad. I mean, I so totally DON'T like him anymore.

POLONIUS: Good! *(POLONIUS exits)*

OPHELIA: *(OPHELIA to audience)* I'm a teenager, like I'm going to listen to my dad!

(OPHELIA exits)

ACT 1 SCENES 4 & 5

(HAMLET, HORATIO, and MARCELLUS enter)

MARCELLUS: *(to the audience)* Something is rotten in the state of Denmark.

HAMLET: Okay, I'm here. Now, where is this ghost of my dad you have been talking about?

(HORATIO and MARCELLUS are looking around; GHOST enters)

HORATIO and MARCELLUS: There he is!

HAMLET: Where?

(GHOST sneaks up behind HAMLET)

GHOST: Boo!

HAMLET: Aghhhhh!

GHOST: Hah! Scared ya!

HAMLET: Who are you?

GHOST: *(in a ghostly voice)* I am your father's spirit.

HAMLET: Oh. ….What!?

GHOST: Your father. You know, the ex-King! I want you to know that the serpent that did sting thy father's life now wears his crown.

HAMLET: What?

GHOST: I was the King until your Uncle Claudius poisoned me by pouring icky stuff in my ear! Murder most foul!

HAMLET: Uncle Claudius killed you?

GHOST: Yeah, then he married my wife, YOUR MOM, and then became King!

HAMLET: WHAT! Ohhh, that makes me soooo mad!

GHOST: Yeah? Well, how do you think I feel? Dead and all.... O horrible, O horrible, most horrible.

HAMLET: Yeah, guess that stinks, too. So what do you want me to do?

GHOST: First, update the body count. *(HAMLET updates body count)* Then avenge me! You MUST kill Claudius!

HAMLET: Whoa! Kill Claudius? Well…..ahhh….not really sure I like that. I mean, it's just not right, killing someone. What if you don't really exist?

GHOST: Did you not hear me? He killed me, married your mom, and is now the new King. Doesn't that make you a bit angry?

HAMLET: *(getting riled up)* Yeah.

GHOST: I am your father. Don't you want to avenge my death!

HAMLET: *(getting more riled up)* YEAH!

GHOST: Then get going!

HAMLET: I WILL AVENGE YOU, FATHER!

GHOST: Oh, and Hamlet?

HAMLET: YEAH?

GHOST: Boo! *(HAMLET jumps up scared)*

HAMLET: Quit doing that!

GHOST: Sorry, son. It's one of the perks of the job. My hour is almost come, now get going! *(now in a ghostly voice)* AVENGE ME!

(GHOST exits)

HAMLET: *(to exiting ghost)*

Rest, Rest, perturbed spirit!

(to audience)

That one, that Claudius, may smile and smile and be a villain. Hah! I don't think so, not on my watch!

(ALL exit)

ACT 2 SCENE 1

(enter OPHELIA and POLONIUS)

OPHELIA: Dad, Hamlet is looking a bit weird lately. I mean, his clothes are ragged and he is talking to himself… not quite as cute as he once was, but I still like him!

POLONIUS: I told you to stay away from him!

OPHELIA: I did!

POLONIUS: Hamlet is probably crazy without your love! That hath made him mad. *(to audience)* I will tell Claudius the king!

(ALL exit)

ACT 2 SCENE 2

(enter CLAUDIUS, ROSENCRANTZ, GUILDENSTERN, and GERTRUDE)

CLAUDIUS: Rosencrantz and Guildenstern?

ROSENCRANTZ & GUILDENSTERN: Yes sir!

CLAUDIUS: I need you to take on a very, very, very, very, very, very secret mission!

ROSENCRANTZ: Secret mission? Yes sir!

GUILDENSTERN: We get to be spies?

ROSENCRANTZ: I want to be the spy!

GUILDENSTERN: *(starting an argument with ROSENCRANTZ)* No, I'm the spy!

ROSENCRANTZ: NO, I'm the spy!

GUILDENSTERN: NO! I'M THE SPY!

CLAUDIUS: Stop!

ROSENCRANTZ & GUILDENSTERN: Sorry, sir.

GUILDENSTERN: *(whispering to ROSENCRANTZ)* I'm still the spy!

GERTRUDE: We need you to find out why Hamlet is acting so strange lately. I beseech you instantly to visit my too much changed son, Hamlet.

GUILDENSTERN: We will do whatever it takes.

ROSENCRANTZ: *(starting an argument with GUILDENSTERN)* Hey, that's my line.

GUILDENSTERN: No, it's my line.

ROSENCRANTZ: No, It's MY line!

GUILDENSTERN: NO, IT'S MY LINE!!!

CLAUDIUS: Stop!

ROSENCRANTZ & GUILDENSTERN: Sorry, sir.

ROSENCRANTZ: By the way, is there any money in it for us?

CLAUDIUS: Sure, here's a dollar.

ROSENCRANTZ: *(takes dollar)* It's mine!

GUILDENSTERN: *(starting an argument with ROSENCRANTZ)* No, it's mine!

ROSENCRANTZ: No, mine!

GUILDENSTERN: NO! MINE!

CLAUDIUS: *(annoyed by them)* Here's another dollar, just go!

(ROSENCRANTZ & GUILDENSTERN exit, still arguing; enter POLONIUS)

POLONIUS: *(to CLAUDIUS)* Sir, I have found the very cause of Hamlet's lunacy. I know why he has been acting so crazy!

GERTRUDE: Why!?

POLONIUS: I will be brief, since brevity is the soul of wit, your noble son is mad. Looney. Bonkers, I tell you! He is in love with Ophelia and I have told her to reject him! Claudius, why don't we spy on him?

CLAUDIUS: Sounds like fun! But what if he is faking being crazy?

POLONIUS: Hmmm. Though this be madness, yet there is method in't.

CLAUDIUS: Right?

(exit CLAUDIUS, POLONIUS, and GERTRUDE)

(enter HAMLET, ROSENCRANTZ, and GUILDENSTERN)

ROSENCRANTZ: What's up, Ham?

GUILDENSTERN: How have you been, buddy?

HAMLET: Oh, just thinking.

ROSENCRANTZ: 'Bout what?

HAMLET: Well, since you asked. Did you know there is nothing either good or bad, but thinking makes it so?

GUILDENSTERN: *(ROSENCRANTZ & GUILDENSTERN looking at each other with a puzzled look on their faces)* Man, you are a weird dude.

HAMLET: Whatever. What brings you around here?

ROSENCRANTZ: My lord, we were sent for, by the king. Oh look, here comes some players.

PLAYER 1: Hello. We are the players.

PLAYER 2: Here to do a play!

HAMLET: *(to audience)* Ah haa! I have an idea!

The play's the thing.

Wherein I'll catch the conscience of the king.

I will have the players act out how my father was killed! Then Claudius will feel guilty and admit his crime! Oh, vengeance!

Claudius is a bloody, bawdy villain!

Remorseless, treacherous, lecherous, kindless villain!

(to PLAYERS) Soooo, what if I said I could get you in front of the king?

PLAYER 1: Sounds great!

HAMLET: OK, but you have to do a special play that I write. You good with that?

PLAYER 2: Great! Let's go!

(ALL exit but HAMLET, who addresses audience)

HAMLET: What luck to find these actors! It will be great to see Claudius show his guilt! What a piece of work is a man!

(HAMLET exits)

ACT 3 SCENE 1

(enter HAMLET)

HAMLET: To be, or not to be, that is the question. *(to audience)* Really…that IS the question, and if any of you have the answer, I would really appreciate a little help here.

(enter OPHELIA)

OPHELIA: Hello, Ham.

HAMLET: Hello, O.

OPHELIA: So, whatcha been up to?

HAMLET: Just contemplating life and talking to myself again. Listen to this: To die, to sleep; To sleep, perchance to dream.

OPHELIA: Wow… how romantic.

HAMLET: Hey, you know I like you?

OPHELIA: Really?

HAMLET: Ahhhh, no.

OPHELIA: You are sooooo mean!

HAMLET: I don't like you at all! Get thee to a nunnery!

OPHELIA: O, woe is me! *(OPHELIA exits as she is crying with a really bad fake cry)*

HAMLET: Whatever. Now let me think of another great speech. Oh yeah, *(as HAMLET exits)* What dreams may come, when we blah, blah, blah…..

(HAMLET exits)

ACT 3 SCENE 2

(enter HAMLET, PLAYERS, and HORATIO)

PLAYER 2: *(to Hamlet)* We will do the play just as you wrote it!

PLAYER 1: Do I really have to die?

PLAYER 2: Yes!

PLAYER 1: Do I get to do a great swordfight and die like a brave knight?

PLAYER 2: Ahhhh, no. You die in your sleep.

PLAYER 1: What!?!? Come on, man. That stinks!

PLAYER 2: Just do it. That's what the script says.

PLAYER 1: Fine, but just be warned: this may be the BEST sleep death you have EVER seen!

PLAYER 2: Fine. Let's go.

(PLAYERS off to side practicing their acting)

HAMLET: Horatio, now watch Claudius closely during the play. He will show his guilt and that will prove he killed my father! Hey, guys. *(to the PLAYERS)* Suit the action to the word, the word to the action.

PLAYERS 1&2: Right!

HORATIO: Ahh, you do realize this is a tragedy, right?

HAMLET: Yeah, why?

HORATIO: Well, I just want you to know, that usually, in a tragedy, the main character gets killed in the end.

HAMLET: So what's your point?

HORATIO: YOU are the main character. They even named the play after you, "HAMLET," so BE CAREFUL!

HAMLET: *(getting a little crazy)* Yeah, well, I MUST PROVE HE KILLED MY FATHER!

HORATIO: Okey-dokey. Don't say I didn't warn ya. Here they come!

(enter CLAUDIUS, GERTRUDE, OPHELIA, ROSENCRANTZ & GUILDENSTERN; they sit around to watch the play)

PLAYER 2: We are about to do a tragedy.

ROSENCRANTZ: Like we haven't seen one of those before! *(GUILDENSTERN laughs at the joke)*

PLAYER 1: I am the king!

PLAYER 2: I am your brother.

PLAYER 1: I am tired, I think I will take a nap. *(starts snoring very loudly)*

PLAYER 2: I will kill him by pouring poison in his ear! Muahahaha!!!

(PLAYER 1 dies melodramatically)

PLAYER 2: *(triumphantly)* I am now the king!

CLAUDIUS: *(gets up very angrily)* STOP! Give me some light, away! Everyone, go home!

(ALL exit but HAMLET and HORATIO)

HAMLET: I was right! *(does a happy dance)*

HORATIO: Looks like it.

(HAMLET off to the side to the audience)

HAMLET: I need to see my mother! I will speak daggers to her but use none. I am MAD! MAD I tell you!!!!

(ALL exit; HAMLET exits, madly screaming about being mad)

ACT 3 SCENE 3

(enter CLAUDIUS)

CLAUDIUS: *(to audience)* I feel reallllllllly bad about killing my brother, King Hamlet. I think I will pray about it. Yeah, that will make me feel better! *(he kneels and starts praying; enter HAMLET)*

HAMLET: *(seeing CLAUDIUS and addressing audience)* What's this! *(starts pulling out his sword)* And now I'll do it! And so I am revenged! But he can't fight back, so it's not fair. Oh, darn it! I hate having a conscience, it's so inconvenient! I am so confused!

(exits)

CLAUDIUS: *(to audience)* Well, I don't know about you, but I feel refreshed!

(exits)

ACT 3 SCENE 4

(enter GERTRUDE and POLONIUS)

GERTRUDE: What's up, Polonius?

POLONIUS: I am going to hide and spy on your conversation with Hamlet!

GERTRUDE: Oh, okay.

(POLONIUS hides somewhere; enter HAMLET very mad, swinging his sword around)

HAMLET: MOM!!! I AM VERY MAD!

GERTRUDE: Ahhh! You scared me!

(POLONIUS sneezes from hiding spot)

HAMLET: *(not seeing POLONIUS)* How now, a rat? Who's hiding? *(stabs POLONIUS)*

POLONIUS: Seriously, again? *(they both nod)* Fine! O, I am slain! Ohhhh, the pain! *(updates his own body count, then dies)*

GERTRUDE: Oh me, what has thou done?

HAMLET: Oops, I thought that was Claudius. Hmph, oh well, he was just a fishmonger anyway… as I was saying, I AM MAD you married uncle Claudius!

GERTRUDE: Oh that. Yeah, sorry. *(in a motherly voice)* Now, you just killed Polonius. Clean up this mess and go to your room!

HAMLET: Okay, Mom. *(mimicking his mom in her voice)* Clean up this mess and go to your room.

(ALL exit; HAMLET gets POLONIUS' body offstage)

ACT 4 SCENES 1-3

(enter GERTRUDE and CLAUDIUS)

GERTRUDE: Ahhh, Dear?

CLAUDIUS: Yeah?

GERTRUDE: Ummmm, you would not believe what I have seen tonight! Polonius is dead.

CLAUDIUS: WHAT!?

GERTRUDE: Yeah, Hamlet was acting a little crazy, Polonius sneezed or something, then Hamlet yelled, "A rat, a rat!" and then WHACK! It was over.

CLAUDIUS: *(yelling offstage)* Rosencrantz and Guildenstern!

(enter ROSENCRANTZ & GUILDENSTERN out of breath)

ROSENCRANTZ & GUILDENSTERN: Yes sir!

CLAUDIUS: *(looking worried)* Hamlet! HAMLET! He killed Polonius!

ROSENCRANTZ: Wow!

GUILDENSTERN: Are you sure? I mean, Hamlet seems nice.

CLAUDIUS: What?! Yes, I am sure! Now, I want you to bring him here. I pray you haste in this.

ROSENCRANTZ & GUILDENSTERN: *(confused)* What?

CLAUDIUS: NOW!

ROSENCRANTZ & GUILDENSTERN: *(still confused)* Okay.

(ROSENCRANTZ & GUILDENSTERN run offstage and return with HAMLET)

CLAUDIUS: *(very casual)* Hey, what's up?

HAMLET: What noise, who calls on Hamlet? What do you want?

CLAUDIUS: Now Hamlet. Where's Polonius' body?

HAMLET: I'm not telling!

CLAUDIUS: FINE!

ROSENCRANTZ: What have you done, my lord, with the dead body?

GUILDENSTERN: Will you tell us?

HAMLET: *(sarcastically)* Suuuuuurrrrrre. It's over there. *(pointing offstage)* No, over there. *(pointing in another direction)* No! Over there! *(pointing to a random place in the audience)*

(this goes on a while and ROSENCRANTZ & GUILDENSTERN are running crazily after HAMLET'S directions all over the stage and through the audience; HAMLET is laughing at them)

GUILDENSTERN: Will you STOP?! I'm tired.

CLAUDIUS: Where is Polonius?

HAMLET: Oh, all right. Up the stairs and into the lobby. *(points offstage; ROSENCRANTZ & GUILDENSTERN go get POLONIUS' body and gets him onstage)*

CLAUDIUS: Ewe… he's a mess! Hamlet, I am sending you off to England. Rosencrantz and Guildenstern, take him away!

HAMLET: Fine! Farewell, dear Mother. And I'm taking this with me! *(gets POLONIUS' body offstage; ALL exit but CLAUDIUS)*

CLAUDIUS: *(to audience)* I have arranged his execution in England! *(laughs evilly as he exits)* Muahahaha….

ACT 4 SCENE 4

(enter HAMLET, addresses audience – obviously very upset)

HAMLET: I am suddenly feeling very upset! This play is lasting really long. I need to speed this revenge thing up! Don't you all agree? *(audience will quietly answer yes)*

HAMLET: *(yelling backstage)* HEY, DO YOU ALL AGREE?

(everyone answers backstage, "YES!")

(CLAUDIUS pokes his head out)

CLAUDIUS: Ahhh, excuse me, I'm not so sure I agree….

HAMLET: *(pointing sword at CLAUDIUS)* Go away!

(ALL exit)

ACT 4 SCENES 5 – 7

(enter OPHELIA and GERTRUDE)

GERTRUDE: Hey, Ophelia, you feeling okay?

OPHELIA: *(acting a little crazy)* I am really feeling weird right now.

(OPHELIA wandering around stage doing weird and crazy things, mumbling, "Hey non nonny, nonny, hey nonny"; enter CLAUDIUS)

CLAUDIUS: *(staring at OPHELIA)* She is acting really weird. Is she okay?

GERTRUDE: Well think about it: her father just got killed by her boyfriend, whom she just broke up with, yet is still in love with. How would you feel?

CLAUDIUS: Oh, no wonder why she is kind of wacky.

(enter LAERTES, very upset)

LAERTES: Where is this king? *(noticing CLAUDIUS)* WHAT HAPPENED TO MY FATHER, *(noticing OPHELIA acting crazy)* and why is my sister looking so… loony?

GERTRUDE: Well, as I was telling Claudius, she's a bit bummed that her boyfriend killed your dad.

LAERTES: Aghhhhhhh!!! I will have REVENGE!

CLAUDIUS: Laertes, my friend. Look, I will help you get your revenge. I pray you go with me.

(GERTRUDE and OPHELIA exit; SAILOR brings a letter to CLAUDIUS)

SAILOR: There's a letter for you sir. It says, "Hamlet is returning!" *(SAILOR shows letter that says, "Hamlet is returning!"; SAILOR exits)*

CLAUDIUS: Listen, Hamlet killed your father and wants to kill you too!

LAERTES: Ohhhh, he thinks so! I will get him!

CLAUDIUS: Let's make an evil plan!

LAERTES: Sounds great!

(CLAUDIUS and LAERTES laugh evilly together)

CLAUDIUS: How about you and Hamlet have a sword fight? And Hamlet's sword is blunt?

LAERTES: Great! And I will put poison on my tip to make sure he dies!

CLAUDIUS: Great! And I will put poison in his drink if none of that works!

LAERTES & CLAUDIUS: GREAT!

(they high-five; enter GERTRUDE)

GERTRUDE: What are you two up to?

LAERTES & CLAUDIUS: Nothing. *(laughing to each other)*

GERTRUDE: Well then, ahhh, Laertes? I have some bad news.

LAERTES: Really? I have had enough of that. Can I have some good news?

GERTRUDE: Nope. Ophelia just drowned. *(GERTRUDE gets OPHELIA'S body on stage – head soaking wet if possible!)*

LAERTES: WHAT!? Drown'd! O, where?

GERTRUDE: Yeah, outside…in water…sorry.

LAERTES: Alas, then, she is drown'd?

OPHELIA: *(looks up at audience)* Drowned!

GERTRUDE: Drown'd, drown'd.

LAERTES: I am sooooo going to get Hamlet!!!!

(LAERTES runs offstage, waving his sword; ALL exit; GERTRUDE gets OPHELIA offstage and updates body count)

ACT 5 SCENE 1

(enter GRAVE DIGGERS; HAMLET and HORATIO are off to the side, watching gravediggers)

GRAVE DIGGER 1: You know, I really have to get a better job! Digging graves is no way to make a living! Get it? Graves – living? *(starts laughing to himself)*

GRAVE DIGGER 2: Yeah. I get that your jokes are really bad. Oh, look what I found, a skull from this grave called Yorick.

(HAMLET jumps up and grabs skull; GRAVE DIGGERS exit)

HAMLET: Alas, poor Yorick! I knew him, Horatio.

HORATIO: Really? Well, I think he's dead now.

HAMLET: When I was a kid, he was the jester, the funniest guy I knew.

HORATIO: Yeah? A fellow of infinite jest, well, he's still dead.

HAMLET: So full of life and now he's…..

HORATIO: Dead. *(body count is updated)*

HAMLET: Bummer.

(enter LAERTES, GERTRUDE, and CLAUDIUS)

HORATIO: Oh look! Hide! *(HAMLET and HORATIO go off to side of stage)*

GERTRUDE: We must bury Ophelia. Sweets to the sweet, farewell!

LAERTES: *(starts weeping and crying extremely loud)* I AM SOOOOO MAD AT HAMLET!!! It's his fault my sister and father are dead!

(HAMLET jumps up to confront LAERTES)

HAMLET: Laertes, I loved Ophelia. How dare you say I killed her!

LAERTES: Aghhhhhh! *(charges at HAMLET and they start to fight)*

HORATIO: Hamlet, we must leave.

(HORATIO pulls back HAMLET and exits with him as HAMLET is still yelling at LAERTES; CLAUDIUS pulls back LAERTES)

(ALL exit)

ACT 5 SCENE 2

(enter HAMLET and HORATIO)

HAMLET: Horatio, did you know that Rosencrantz and Guildenstern were taking me to England to have me killed!?

HORATIO: Really?

HAMLET: Yeah, but I got them!

HORATIO: What did you do?

HAMLET: I tricked England into thinking that Rosencrantz and Guildenstern were to be killed.

(enter ROSENCRANTZ & GUILDENSTERN)

ROSENCRANTZ: WHAT?!

GUILDENSTERN: We're dead?

HAMLET: Yep!

ROSENCRANTZ & GUILDENSTERN: *(looking at each other)* Well that stinks. *(both suddenly die dramatically on stage; HAMLET laughs to himself, then updates body count; enter OSRIC, stepping over bodies)*

HAMLET: Osric! What brings you here?

OSRIC: The king has placed a wager that you can not beat Laertes in a swordfight!

HAMLET: What!?! Bring it on!

HORATIO: I don't know, man, this doesn't seem right. I will tell him you are not fit.

HAMLET: *(to OSRIC)* Tell him I will fight!

(exit OSRIC)

HORATIO: I'm telling you. This is a TRAGEDY, remember? The central theme ALL NIGHT! You shouldn't fight! You will lose, my lord.

HAMLET: I don't think so. The time is NOW!

(enter LAERTES, GERTRUDE, OSRIC, CLAUDIUS, and other on-lookers)

HAMLET: So, I hear you want to fight?

LAERTES: Yeah, you killed my father... and sister. Prepare to die!

HAMLET: Look, I really didn't mean to kill your father. He sneezed and freaked me out.

LAERTES: *(handing sword to HAMLET)* Just take your sword and let's go.

(CLAUDIUS and LAERTES to the side)

CLAUDIUS: Is your sword poisoned?

LAERTES: Yep. Is your wine poisoned?

CLAUDIUS: You betcha!

HORATIO: *(to HAMLET)* Listen, this doesn't seem right....

CLAUDIUS: *(to audience, while all watch him)* If Hamlet wins, we will all drink wine! *(winks at audience while holding up poisoned wine cup)*

(LAERTES and HAMLET start to fight; HAMLET strikes first)

LAERTES: Ouch! That hurt!

HAMLET: How about this! *(strikes him again)*

LAERTES: Hey! *(strikes back and hits HAMLET)*

HAMLET: Ouch!

GERTRUDE: All this fighting is making me thirsty! *(drinks poisoned wine)*

CLAUDIUS: GERTRUDE, do not drink! *(to audience)* It is the poisoned cup. It is too late. Oh well.

(during fight, HAMLET and LAERTES manage to drop and switch swords – this must be obvious to the audience)

LAERTES: *(to CLAUDIUS)* He has MY SWORD!

CLAUDIUS: Well, don't get hit!

(HAMLET strikes LAERTES again)

LAERTES: Nooooooooo!!!!!!!

(GERTRUDE suddenly gets up and starts to die)

HAMLET: MOMMY!!!! Aghhhhhhh!!!!

GERTRUDE:

O my dear Hamlet.

The drink, the drink! I am poison'd.

(dies in melodramatic fashion, all watch)

HAMLET: *(very mad)*

Oh villainy! Ho, let the door be lock'd!

Treachery! Seek it out!

(LAERTES starts dying)

LAERTES: Hamlet, listen. Claudius poisoned the wine cup and your mom drank it. He also poisoned my sword.

HAMLET: Oh, that's not good.

HORATIO: I told you so!

LAERTES: Nope, we're both going to die.

The king, the king's to blame.

I am justly killed with my own treachery!

(LAERTES falls over dead)

CLAUDIUS: *(to audience)* Don't you just hate tattletales!

HAMLET: CLAUDIUS!!!! *(HAMLET chases CLAUDIUS around stage and finally kills him)*

HAMLET: *(enter FORTINBRAS and some of his men; HAMLET, starting to die)* Well this did not turn out as I expected! I guess this was a tragedy after all! Fortinbras, you are now the king.

O, I die. The rest is silence.

(HAMLET dies melodramatically)

FORTINBRAS: Sweet, I get to be king! *(does a happy dance)* I like tragedies! This place is a mess! Let's see... *(does a body count while stepping over bodies then updates body count)* Oh look, Rosencrantz and Guildenstern are dead, too. *(ALL exit except dead bodies; NARRATOR walks in, stepping over bodies and takes spot at center stage)*

EPILOGUE

NARRATOR: Well, we hope you have enjoyed our show tonight, and the moral is: don't get caught in a Shakespearean tragedy! Especially me. I died, what, four times today? Who writes this stuff? Anyway, we will leave you with this parting thought: Never was a story of more woe, than this of Juliet and her Romeo… and Caesar… and Macbeth…

HAMLET: *(to audience)* And Hamlet!

CLAUDIUS: And me!

GERTRUDE: And me, too!

LAERTES: Hey, don't forget about me!

ROSENCRANTZ & GUILDENSTERN: Don't forget about us!

NARRATOR: Farewell!

(ALL exit)

The End

ABOUT THE AUTHOR

BRENDAN P. KELSO came to writing modified Shakespeare scripts when he was taking time off from work to be at home with his newly born son. "It just grew from there". Within months, he was being asked to offer classes in various locations and acting organizations along the Central Coast of California. Originally employed as an engineer, Brendan never thought about writing. However, his unique personality, humor, and love for engaging kids with The Bard has led him to leave the engineering world and pursue writing as a new adventure in life! He has always believed, "the best way to learn is to have fun!" Brendan makes his home on the Central Coast of California and loves to spend time with his wife and kids.

Made in the USA
Monee, IL
11 August 2025